# THE HITTING CLINIC

# THE HITTING CLINIC

**John Stewart**

**Illustrations by George Henry**

BURFORD BOOKS

Printed in the United States of America

10 9 8 7 6 5 4 3 2 1

Library of Congress Cataloging-in-Publication Data
Stewart, John, 1964–
The hitting clinic / John Stewart.
p. cm.
Includes index.
ISBN 1-58080-131-5 (pbk.)
1. Batting (Baseball)—Training. I. Title.
GV869.S694 2005
796.357'26—dc22 2005001153

# CONTENTS

# INTRODUCTION

It has been said many times that hitting a pitched ball is the hardest thing to do in sports. At any level, a good hitter has success only 30% of the time. This percentage is misleading, because a good hitter will make contact closer to 70% of the time, but only 30% of those touches will be hits where the hitter reaches base. In ten at-bats, a good hitter will hit three balls for hits, two other balls will be hit hard and caught by the defense, and the other five will be hit softly or will be swings with no contact. The fact that a pitcher is throwing the ball off a hill, constantly changing speeds, to a hitter who is attempting to hit the ball with a round bat, allows the hitter very little room for error.

Hitters must have a combination of skills to be successful. They must have strength, timing, technique, concentration, hand-eye coordination, and aggressiveness. A lack of any one of these will result in a less successful hitter.

Learning the proper technique is the first step to becoming a successful hitter. The following pages will explain the basic skills, drills and mechanics required to hit the pitched ball with regularity. Even after learning and understanding this book, however, remember that there is no shortcut for practice. A regular routine of practice to master the skills of hitting is a must. Above all, stay positive both in practice and in the game, because even a good hitter will fail more often than succeed.

# 1

# Getting Ready

Here is the sequence of what happens when a ball is hit. In the pages that follow, we will be discussing each of these steps in detail.

The pitcher is on the mound, looking in at the catcher, preparing to pitch the ball. You are in your stance. Hands are in position and the bat is set. Your eyes should be looking directly at the pitcher. You need to be relaxed and focused on hitting the ball, and hitting it hard. As the pitcher starts the motion, your focus should move, from looking at the pitcher, to the release point the pitcher uses. The pitcher's arm is approaching the release point, and you get ready to start the swing. As the ball is released, try to read the rotation. Is this a fastball or not? Try to decide if the pitch is a strike or a ball. As the pitch is released, start the trigger. Get the hands moving back to the loaded position.

With the trigger starting the swing, pick the front foot up and shift the weight to the back leg. Stride to the pitcher. As the front foot comes to rest on the ground, rotate the back foot and get the bat into the strike zone. Keep the hands close to the body and make the bat track short and direct. The idea is to keep the eye on the ball and the barrel of the bat under control.

The ball is approaching the contact area, and it is a strike. Keep the front shoulder pointed at the pitcher, and get the barrel of the bat to the contact area to meet the pitched ball. As the ball hits the bat, keep your eye on the ball and swing the bat through the ball. As the ball leaves the bat, continue the swing until the body stops the bat. Drop the bat and become a runner.

# Choosing a Bat

Without the correct bat, a hitter will struggle to make contact. A bat that is too heavy or too light will change the way a hitter attempts to swing at the pitch. Getting familiar with the different parts of the bat, as well as the proper size and weight, will pay big dividends when you step into the batter's box.

Before picking the proper bat we should first describe the parts of the bat. The knob of the bat is the very bottom. The bottom of a wooden bat usually has a number, representing the length of the bat, pressed into the bottom of the knob. Normally, there is only one number pressed into the bottom. For instance, a 2 pressed into the bottom means the bat is a 32-inch long bat. A 4 means the bat is 34 inches long. Because players do not use bats longer than 35 inches long, a 7-8-9 or 0 at the bottom normally signifies 27-28-29 or 30 inches in length. The wood bat does not state the weight of the bat, but the wood bat is never more than three ounces lighter than the length. A 33-inch bat would normally be 31 ounces, but on occasion the hitter may find a 33-inch bat with a weight of 30 ounces.

On aluminum bats the length and weight are printed on the barrel of the bat. The barrel is the thickest part of the bat, used to make contact with the ball. The barrel is often referred to as the bat "head," and is about two-and-a-half inches thick. In the middle of the barrel is an area called the "sweet spot." This spot is the area on the barrel that the ball will travel the best when making contact with the pitched ball. This spot is not formally marked, but on contact the hitter will know they have hit the ball there. Normally a bat's sweet spot is three to four inches in length and about halfway from the label to the end of the bat. An aluminum bat's sweet spot is larger than that of a wood bat, sometimes as much as five inches long.

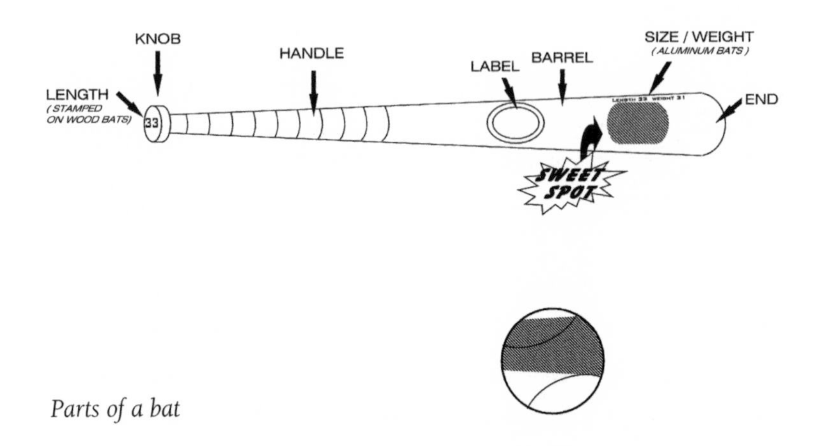


*Parts of a bat*

The oval label on the wood bat shows the manufacturer's name and represents the start of the hitting area for that particular bat. The label on the wood bat is more visible than on the aluminum bat, where often there is no label at all. The section below the label is referred to as the handle. Hitting the ball on the handle is not recommended—it will result in very little power and many broken wooden bats. On the aluminum bat, the hit on the handle will sting the hands of the hitter.

A hitter very often overlooks picking the proper-sized bat. Not all bats are the same, and the length and weight of the bat will affect the success a hitter will have. A heavy bat will not allow the hitter to get the bat in the strike zone in time to hit the pitched ball, because it slows the bat speed and causes the hitter to swing late. A successful hitter usually wants to wait as long as possible on the decision to swing or let the pitch go. A bat that is too heavy forces the hitter to start the swing early, often resulting in a swing at a bad pitch.

A successful hitter will be able to control the bat and be able to adjust the bat to make solid contact on the barrel. A bat that is too long or too heavy will create problems for the hitter who is trying to make adjustments as the pitch approaches the plate. The velocity that a pitcher is throwing will also affect the decision on the weight of the bat a hitter should use. If the pitcher is throwing very hard, a lighter bat may be necessary to have success against the fastball.

Length is another consideration when choosing the proper bat. Unlike weight, there are simple guidelines for getting the correct bat length. Pick a bat that is long enough to cover the strike zone. If your stance leaves you far from the plate, a longer bat is needed to reach the outside corner of the strike zone. If standing close to the plate is more comfortable, a shorter bat is fine. Most often the length of the bat is based on the length of the hitter's arms. A hitter with short arms will need a longer bat, and the hitter with long arms can use a shorter bat and still cover the strike zone. A bat that is too long will make it very hard for the hitter to hit the ball on the sweet spot, because the sweet spot is so far away from the hitter's eyes. Given all of this, the proper weight of the bat is still much more important than the proper length.

One other note to keep in mind when deciding on the right bat is the style of hitter you are. A line-drive gap hitter with limited power should find a bat slightly heavier so the ball will travel farther at contact. The speed the bat generates when reaching the contact area is an important factor, so find the bat that can be easily swung and controlled. If the hitter is constantly hitting the ball foul to the pull field (a right-handed hitter hitting the ball foul to left field, or a left-handed hitter hitting the ball foul to right field), the bat may be too light. If the ball is hit to the opposite field on a regular basis, the bat may be too heavy.

If the bats available are too long or too heavy, choking up is an option. Choking up means to grip the bat higher up, instead of at the bottom of the handle at the knob. Holding the bat higher up the handle will shorten the bat and make the bat lighter, because the hitter is not swinging the entire bat.

The velocity a pitcher is throwing may also factor in when deciding to choke up on the bat. If a pitcher has a good fastball the hitter may decide to choke up to lighten the bat. If a pitcher is ahead in the count, a hitter may choke up, making the bat shorter so hitter will have more control and be better able to make contact.

Make sure you choose a bat that can be swung with ease. Bat speed is a very important factor when hitting a pitched ball. If in doubt on the proper bat, pick the lighter one.

## The Grip

Attempting to swing the bat with an incorrect grip will often cause the hitter to swing and miss. The grip also affects the way a hitter generates bat speed. Knowing the proper way to hold the bat will greatly help a hitter make contact.

A bat handle should not be squeezed—hands should be relaxed on the bat. The hands should grip the bat much like holding an axe. To identify the proper grip, put the end of the bat on the ground with the knob of the bat resting on the hitter's thigh. Then slide your fingers under the handle with you fingertips touching the handle. From here, wrap your fingers around the bat loosely. This should be the grip of the bat. As you pick the bat up, look to see if the top hand's large knuckles are lined up with your bottom hand's small knuckles. Very often a hitter will grip the bat with the large knuckles of both hands aligned with each other, causing the bat to be too far back in the hand, which limits the flexibility of the hitter's wrists. A bat rested too far back in the hands will not allow the hitter to throw the hands at the ball with the accuracy and the speed needed to be effective. Conversely, holding the bat too far onto the fingertips will cause the hitter to lose control of the bat and will greatly reduce the strength a hitter can generate during the swing. Often with the grip well out on the fingertips, the bat will fly out of the hitter's hands, causing a dangerous situation for players and spectators.

*Proper grip*

If done correctly, the handle should rest on the pad of the top hand. If you were to open up your hands in the grip we have discussed, the bat should be resting on the middle of your fingers. This is the correct grip of the bat.

Be sure your hands are in contact with each other. There should be no distance between the top of your bottom hand and the bottom of the top hand. If there is any space between the hands the freedom of the wrists to swing is greatly limited. Occasionally, a big strong hitter with a light bat may find it more comfortable to leave the pinky of the bottom hand off the bottom of the knob. This is fine if the hitter is strong enough to swing the bat and keep control during the swing.

## Box Placement

Standing at the wrong position in the batter's box will limit the area in which a hitter can make contact. A good hitter must be able to cover the entire plate.

The batter's box is three feet wide and six feet long, leaving a lot of area for the hitter to set up. The inside line of the box is six inches from home plate. The plate is 17 inches wide. Given all these measurements, a batter standing on the inside line of the batter's box is 23 inches from the outside corner of the plate. If the hitter is swinging a 33-inch bat, there is plenty of room for error. A hitter's job is to have plate coverage, the ability to reach any pitch that crosses the plate in the strike zone. A hitter with long arms can stand further from the plate than a hitter with short arms. Likewise, a hitter with a longer bat can stand further away from the plate than the hitter using the shorter bat.

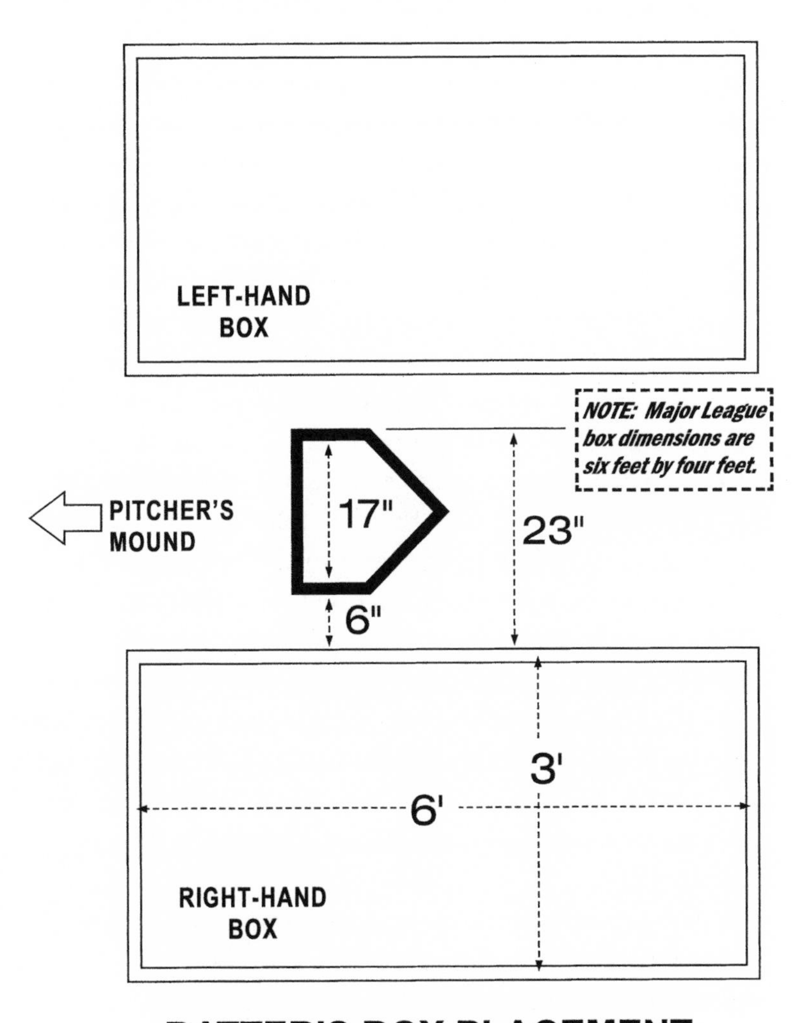


*The batter's box*

Being able to reach the outside corner of the plate is the most important element to keep in mind when positioning yourself in the box. Pitchers will throw most pitches on or near the outside portion of the plate. The best position for the hitter is to be able to reach the outside corner of the plate with the bat extending slightly over the outside edge. If a hitter stands in a position where they cannot cover the entire plate, it allows the pitcher to have an advantage, because the pitcher now has an area of the plate that cannot be hit.

Positioning yourself forward or back in the batter's box also has different effects. Standing in the very front of the batter's box will allow the hitter less time to see the pitch. This hitter will have to make a swing decision earlier than the hitter standing at the back of the batter's box. The advantage to standing in the front of the box, however, is the ability to hit a breaking pitch before it starts its maximum break. Standing in the middle of the box will allow more time to see the ball. This position in the box will also allow the hitter to make contact with the curve or slider before it gets to maximum break. Standing deep in the box will give the maximum amount of time to see the ball, but the hitter will be forced to hit off-speed pitches at their maximum break.

A hitter who starts in the back portion of the batter's box is said to be "standing deep" in the box. The hitter standing in the front of the box is referred to as "standing up" in the box. The rules state that a hitter can stand anywhere in the box as long as both feet are inside the marked area, or are in contact with the white chalk line that marks the outside edges of the batter's box. A hitter cannot stand with one or both feet outside of the batter's box or without contact with the lines. A hitter cannot make a swing that causes one or both feet to leave the batter's box at contact. At contact, both feet have to be inside the box.

Hitters should find a spot in the batter's box that will allow them to swing comfortably at the outside corner, while also being able to see the pitched ball long enough to make a good decision on whether the pitch is a strike or a ball. To decide where to position yourself, first stand in the middle of the box with the bat held in the proper grip. Start a normal swing in slow motion. As the bat reaches the area over the plate, stop the swing. At this point, the bat should be extended out over the plate in the strike zone. Drop the bat from your hand and let it hit the ground. Notice if the bat covers the entire plate, or if the outside edge of the plate is too far for the bat to reach a pitch in that area. If the bat covers the plate, and extends no more than one to two inches over the outside corner, the distance from the plate is correct. If the bat does not reach the outside portion of the plate, move in slightly toward the plate and try this test again.

## The Stance

A correct stance is the start of a successful swing. A hitter whose body is in a poor position will struggle to make a good swing and maintain balance.

Of all the mechanics involved in hitting a baseball, the stance is the one with the most variation. There are many different stances a hitter can use. The most important part of the stance is that it is comfortable to the hitter and allows the hitter to cover the entire strike zone with little effort. A hitter must experiment with many different types of stances to find the most effective one.

There are two important parts of a stance—how far apart the feet are at the start of the stance, and how long the stride will be when attempting make contact with the pitched ball. These two parts of the swing work together.

Let's have a look at frequently used stances. In the open stance, the hitter does not have the feet parallel to the plate when setting up. Instead, the hitter has the back foot closer to the inside line of the batter's box, the line closest to the plate. The front foot in an open stance is placed slightly closer to the third base line for the right-handed hitter, and slightly closer to the first base line for the left-handed hitter. This allows the hitter to open the hips when setting up to watch the pitcher throw the pitch.

There are many variations on the open stance, all of which involve how close to the base line the front foot is placed. As discussed earlier, the hitter needs to experiment with different positions of the open stance to find the most comfortable position. A hitter can be very open, meaning his front foot is very much in the direction of the base line, or only slightly open, almost parallel to the base line. The key when working out of the open stance is to be sure that the front foot gets to a good hitting position, striding to the pitcher's belt buckle, when attempting to hit the ball.

The conventional stance is the most common. In this stance the hitter has both feet directly under the body, parallel to the inside line of the batter's box. This stance is the simplest because the hitter only needs to stride forward during the pitch. This stance is also the easiest to keep balanced. The variations in this stance have only to do with the distance the feet are apart. Keep in mind when using the conventional stance that the front foot cannot vary in stride

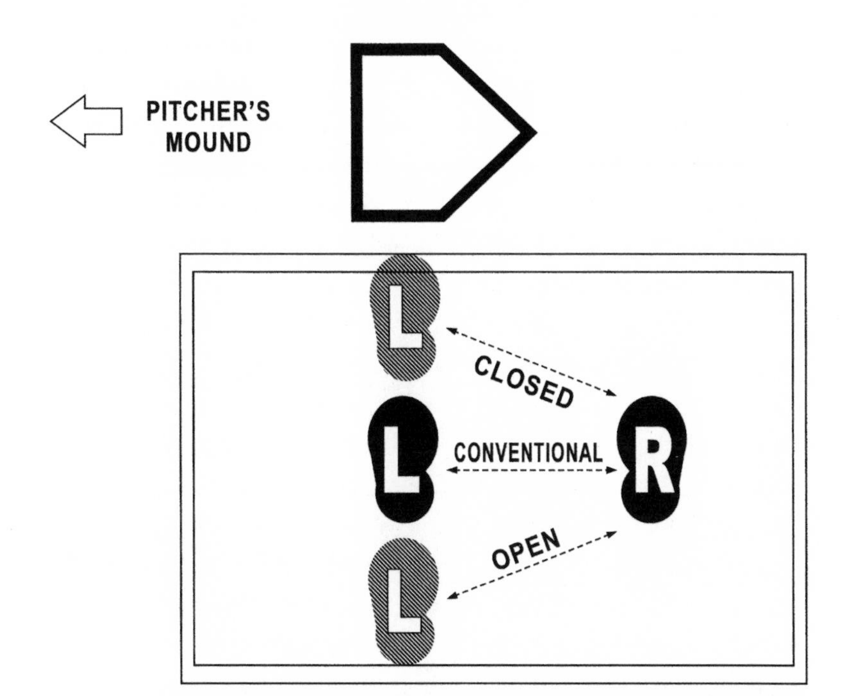


*Batting stances for the right-handed hitter*

direction. The front foot has to stride forward. If the front foot moves in any other direction, the swing will fall apart.

The final stance we will discuss is the closed stance. The closed stance is just the opposite of the open stance. The back foot in this stance is further from the inside line of the batter's box than the front foot. The closed stance allows the hitter to watch the pitcher deliver the ball from over the front shoulder. The hitter having trouble striding correctly often uses the closed stance. The correct stride finds the hitter stepping toward the belt buckle of the pitcher. In this stance, the hitter will be more likely to keep the front shoulder in the proper position at contact. The hitter having trouble hitting the outside pitch will sometimes use this closed stance to aid in reaching the outside pitch with more success.

The closed stance can cause trouble only if the hitter's stride is in the direction of the inside line of the batter's box. The stride needs to be, as in all stances, to the belt buckle of the pitcher. If the stride heads in the direction of the inside line, the hitter will be too close at contact and the bat will not have a clear path to get to the contact area. As with the open stance, there are many variations on the closed stance. A hitter can very closed, where the hitter's back is facing the pitcher. Slightly closed will have the hitter's feet placed almost parallel, with the front foot just a bit closer to the inside line of the batter's box than the back foot.

The upright stance is also a very common approach to hitting. This stance can be combined with the open or closed stance. In the upright stance the hitter stands straight up at the plate. The knees may have just a bit of bend to them, but for the most part the hitter is very erect. A hitter can be tall and closed or tall and open in the stance. The hitter may also choose to use an upright even stance, which is the tall conventional stance.

The other type of stance is the crouch stance, when the hitter is very flexed at the knees. This stance gives the look of the hitter bending down low at the plate. As with the tall stance, this stance can be in combination with the open or closed approach.

The most important thing to remember when setting up at the plate in any stance is *comfort* and *balance*. If a hitter cannot get balanced the stance will be ineffective.

After deciding what stance is most comfortable, take the bat and take a slow-motion practice swing. As the bat is extended over the plate, again drop the bat to the ground. Check to see if the bat covers the entire plate. Always keep in mind that we need to cover the outside corner, regardless of the type of stance and how far the feet are from the plate. Make the necessary adjustment to the stance and distance from the plate to best cover the plate. A stance with plate coverage is the goal, but the hitter needs to also keep in mind that the stance should allow the hitter to see the pitched ball–make sure the stance does not limit the ability to see the pitched ball.

## The Strike Zone

The strike zone is defined as follows: when a batter assumes a natural batting stance at home plate, the strike zone is the space over any part of the 17-inch plate that is above the batter's kneecaps and below the batter's armpits. This is important because the ball may pass the hitter in the strike zone and then be caught by the catcher out of the strike zone, making it look like the pitch was not a strike. The umpire will make a decision on the pitch based on its position when it passes the hitter, not where the catcher catches the ball. When the hitter sets up at the plate awaiting the pitch, the strike zone is now defined. Regardless of whether a hitter bends down to swing, or stands taller to swing, the strike zone does not

*The strike zone*

change. The strike zone is defined as the hitter sets up to hit. The established strike zone cannot vary during that time at bat.

## The Stride

A hitter who cannot perfect the stride will fall victim to balance trouble. A hitter needs to know the type of swing they have, and keep the stride controlled and well integrated with the swing.

There are basically three types of strides. First is the long stride. In the long stride the hitter sets up at the plate with the feet set in the stance, and during the swing the front foot is lifted and moved toward the pitcher more than six to eight inches. Usually, the long stride is used when a hitter has set the feet close together in the stance. If the feet are far apart in the stance a long stride will cause the head to lower during the swing, and the hitter's ability to track the pitched ball is affected. Depending on the size of the hitter, the requirements for a long stride may vary. A very tall hitter may have to stride eight to ten inches before a long stride is achieved.

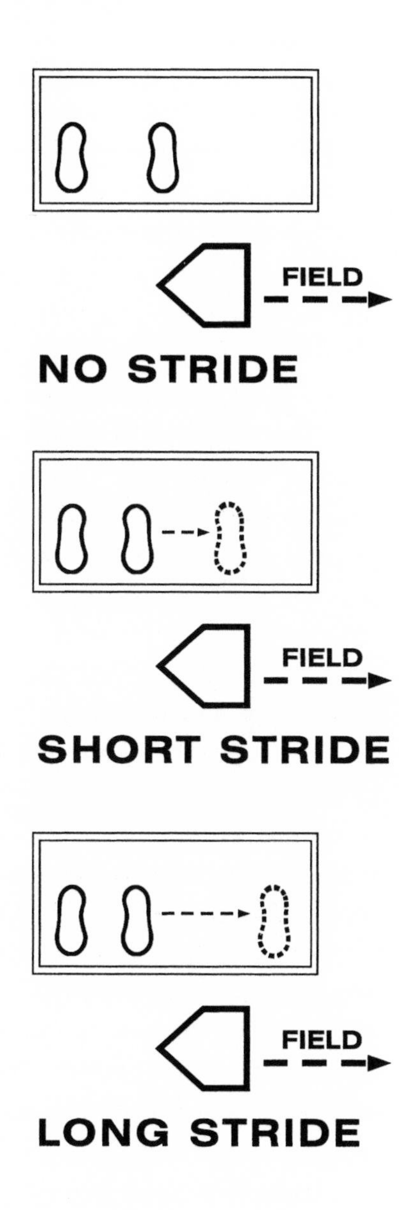


*Three types of strides*

The short stride is used most often when the hitter has a spread stance. This is because the stance is already spread out, so the hitter cannot stride too far. The spread stance is when the feet of the hitter start at least at shoulder-width apart. From the spread stance, the hitter's stride is usually six inches or less. This stride is effective because the hitter spends very little time moving the front foot during the pitch. The front foot is off the ground for very little time, allowing the hitter more time to balance and prepare to hit the ball. The stride needs to be toward the pitcher, or slightly to the plate. Never should the stride be totally in the direction of the plate.

The final type of stride is–no stride at all. This type of approach can only be achieved effectively when the hitter is in the spread conventional stance, because the hitter cannot get any balance into the swing with other stances. Balance will also become a concern if the no stride is used in the close stance. The no stride is exactly as it states–the front foot never moves toward the pitcher. Instead, the front foot is lifted up and returned to the same position during the swing. During the swing the front foot remains in the same position through contact. The only movement out of the front foot is a slight rotation of the toes from pointed at the inside line of the batter's box to the inside front corner of the batter's box. This move is a small rotation, allowing the hitter to rotate the hips during the swing. This type of approach is good for the line-drive hitter, because the swing is normally short and quick with a contact swing as opposed to a big, uppercut homerun-type swing. A hitter who is very good at staying balanced, with good upper-body strength, will also have success with this stride. The no stride allows the hitter to stay back longer and let the power of the pitcher's fastball aid in the power a hitter generates during the swing. The drawback with this type of stride is the lack of lower body action. Because the stride has almost no lower-body rotation, the hitter has to make up the difference with timing and bat control.

Regardless of the type of stride, long or short, the stride needs to be toward the pitcher's belt buckle. In the no stride the stride is eliminated, but the front foot still needs to be planted at the pitcher. Another important point about the stride is that the front stride foot should never leave the toes pointed directly at the pitcher. The toes should point to the front inside corner of the batter's box at the time of contact.

If the hitter's stride is in any other direction, the hitter will have trouble covering the entire strike zone. The hitter that strides to the base line will be unable to hit the ball on the outside corner. The hitter that strides directly to the plate, which is referred to as "driving in," will find many pitches being hit on the handle. This hitter will also have very little luck hitting the inside pitch because the swing will not allow the barrel of the bat to reach the inside pitch.

Remember, comfort and balance should be the main objectives when choosing the stride. Strength and type of hitter should be considerations when developing a proper stride. The short stride and the no stride will allow the hitter more time to look at an off-speed pitch. The long strider will normally have more power because the bottom half will have a bigger role in the swing. The long strider will have less luck with the off-speed stuff because the stride starts earlier, leaving less time to read the pitch and decide if the pitch is a strike or ball.

All strides should be slow and controlled. Quick, rushed or jerked-type strides will cause the hitter's head to move or loss of balance, both of which will result in failure to hit the ball correctly.

## Hand Position

Knowing where the bat and hands should be placed as the swing starts will greatly increase the hitter's ability to make adjustments during the swing. A hitter who does not know the proper hand placement will very often choose the wrong placement for their type of swing. This will result in a swing breakdown. Every hitter needs to match the hand position and bat angle to their type of swing.

There is more than one position that the hands can set up when awaiting the pitched ball. Try to find a position for your hands that allows the bat to get to the contact area successfully. The hand positions that are most common will be discussed here. As always, comfort is the most important aspect when deciding which position to use.

The high hand position is the first position we will discuss. High hands are achieved when the hitter sets the hands above or at shoulder level. With high hands the hitter needs to be sure they are strong enough, and fast enough, to move the hands from the shoulder level to the strike

*High hand position*

zone in time to make solid contact with the pitch. The high-hand hitter will generate much more bat speed and strength in the swing than others. Often, however, the high hand hitter will develop a loop swing, in which the track of the bat starts at the bottom of the strike zone and works upward to the pitched ball. This swing is sure to produce pop-ups, because the bat will make contact with the pitch on the bottom portion of the ball instead of on the upper half of the ball, which is the correct contact position. This high-hand position will normally cause the hitter's swing to be long and more complicated. One other potential problem with the high-hand position is a hand hitch, when the hitter has too much wasted hand action before starting the swing. High-hand hitters often develop a hand hitch prior to starting the swing, resulting in the bat reaching the contact area too late.

The opposite of the high-hand position is the low-hand placement. The low-hand position is achieved when the hands start the hitting process with the hands below the letters on the uniform. The low hand setup is more common with the hitter who hits line drives, or likes to slap the ball. Normally, the smaller or weaker hitter will use this type of hand position because less strength is needed to get

*Low hand position*

the bat to the contact area. The low hand position will produce a flat swing, and will make it easier to get to a low pitch. The problems with this type of hand position are similar to those of the high-hand hitter. A hand hitch will often occur if the hitter is trying to hit home runs out of this hand position. If the hitter in the low-hand position is chasing a high pitch, often the hand hitch will appear. The low-hand hitter will not generate the type of bat speed the high-hand hitter will. The reason for the lack of bat speed is that a hitter with the low hands sets the hands very close to the contact area. Because the hitter's hands are so close to the strike zone, there is no distance in which the hitter can generate bat speed.

The last hand position we will discuss is the letter-high hand position. This hand position is the most popular of all hand positions. As the name implies, the letter-high hand position is very near the letters on the chest of the uniform. The hands should be placed just above the letters near the back armpit. At this position, the hitter has the hands close to the start of the bat track. At this point, the hitter will have to use the least amount of effort to get the bat into the contact area.

*Medium hand position*

The problems that arise with this hand placement have more to do with the hands being improperly positioned on top of each other, rather than problems with bat speed or a hand hitch as in the other positions. The proper position of the hands is to stack them directly on top of each other, just like stacking blocks. The hands should not be tilted back or forward. Hands tilted back will cause a flat swing. The hands being tilted forward, toward the pitcher, will cause a loop swing.

As we discuss the different parts of the swing, you will notice that we always stress the same theory. The hitter must be able to get the bat through the swing to the contact area. The good hitter always gets to the contact area under control and with a proper angle on the bat to make solid contact.

## Bat Angle

Bat angles are a matter of personal preference. As always, comfort and success are the most important factors in deciding the bat angle to use. The bat angle has nothing to do with the type of stance or the hand position. The bat angle may be decided based on the strength of the hitter or the type of swing the hitter is trying to produce.

The tall bat is very popular with the hitter with high hands. The tall bat is the bat that is pointed to the sky, straight up over the back shoulder of the hitter. The bat will have very little or no tilt. With the bat tall, the hands will be stacked directly on top of each other. If the tall bat is tilted slightly forward toward the pitcher it is referred to as a wrap. A bat wrap will often cause a hand hitch. A small

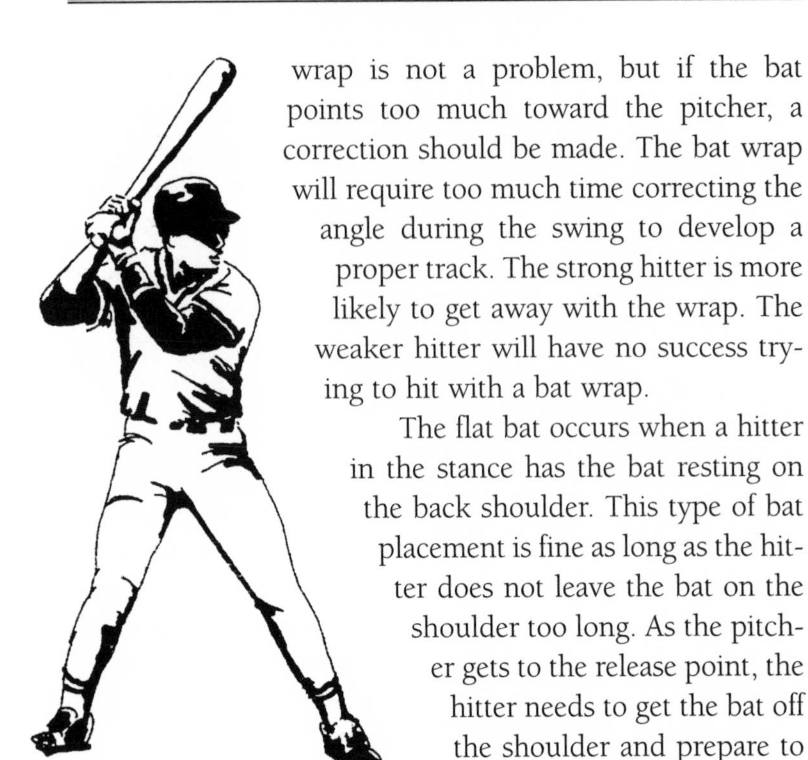
*Tall bat*

wrap is not a problem, but if the bat points too much toward the pitcher, a correction should be made. The bat wrap will require too much time correcting the angle during the swing to develop a proper track. The strong hitter is more likely to get away with the wrap. The weaker hitter will have no success trying to hit with a bat wrap.

The flat bat occurs when a hitter in the stance has the bat resting on the back shoulder. This type of bat placement is fine as long as the hitter does not leave the bat on the shoulder too long. As the pitcher gets to the release point, the hitter needs to get the bat off the shoulder and prepare to swing the bat. Leaving the bat on the shoulder too long will cause the hitter to arrive at the contact area too late. The flat-bat hitter needs to lift the bat slightly off the shoulder as the pitcher goes into the motion. This is referred to as a trigger. (We will discuss the importance of the trigger later.) The important thing to remember with the flat-bat approach is that the bat does not get wrapped behind the hitter's head. Occasionally, the hitter will rest the bat on the shoulder and tilt the head of the bat back behind the hitter's head. Much like the tall-bat hitter, if the bat gets behind the head it will cause a wrap. The wrap will cause the hitter trouble getting the bat started into the bat track.

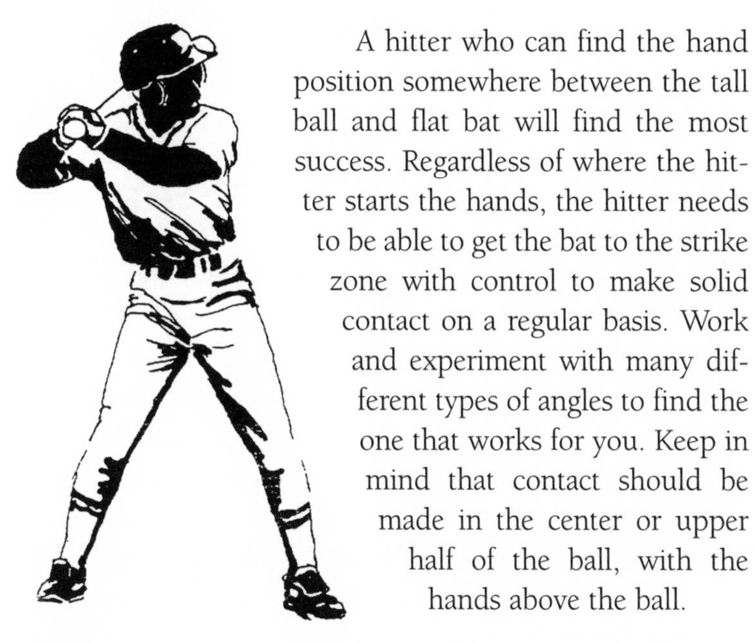

A hitter who can find the hand position somewhere between the tall ball and flat bat will find the most success. Regardless of where the hitter starts the hands, the hitter needs to be able to get the bat to the strike zone with control to make solid contact on a regular basis. Work and experiment with many different types of angles to find the one that works for you. Keep in mind that contact should be made in the center or upper half of the ball, with the hands above the ball.

*Flat bat*

## Elbows, Hands, and Shoulders

A proper swing cannot be performed with coordinating the elbows, hands, and shoulders. A hitter needs to know the correct placement and movement of all these parts. Without a clear understanding of how these parts work together, the swing will fall apart and fail.

As a hitter sets up in the batter's box, first set the feet and grip in the proper position. Now we need to turn our attention to the elbows. It is very common for a young hitter to point the back elbow to the umpire. Very often coaches will yell to the hitter "keep that back elbow up!" This is unfortunately incorrect. The back elbow should be pointed at the catcher—slightly down from the umpire. The back elbow should not be even with the back shoulder in height. If it is too high, it will cause the hitter to wrap the hands and wrist around the bat, putting the hands and the wrists in the wrong position for the swing. If the back elbow is tucked up against the body, the hitter will not have the freedom needed in the swing to generate good bat speed.

The front elbow should be rested pointing to the ground. There should be very little space between the body and the front elbow. A front elbow that is too far from the body and pointed to the pitcher will cause the hands to move into a poor position to hit. This high front elbow will result in a stiff muscle swing, which will make it almost impossible to make adjustments or create bat speed in the swing. The front elbow too close to the body will not allow the hitter to get a proper trigger. With the front elbow resting up against the body, the upper body is locked and cannot move freely.

When the elbows are in position, it is important to remember the hands should be about letter high. If the hands start below the letters, the hitter will very often have a hitch in the swing. This hitch is caused because the hitter will try to adjust the hands up to the letters during the swing. If the hitter starts with the hands at the letters, the adjustment does not need to be made. Hands that are too high at the setup will result in the same problem—during the swing the hitter will need to adjust the hands down. This may not cause a hand hitch, but will cause a long and less effective swing.

A proper swing requires the hitter to keep the front elbow close to the body, not allowing the front elbow to stray more than a couple of inches from the chest. If the

*Proper placement of the front and back elbows, the hands, and the shoulders*

front elbow starts to separate from the body, it will affect the angle at which the bat gets to the strike zone. With this in mind, starting with the front elbow in the proper position should aid in the proper position of the front elbow during the swing. The front elbow that has too much movement in the swing will cause the hitter to develop length in the swing. As we have learned, too much length in a swing will cause the hitter to get to the contact area late, or make it hard to make adjustments because the swing has to start earlier than that of the hitter with a short, compact swing.

If the hitter tenses up during the swing, bat speed and ability to adjust to the pitched ball will be affected. Stay loose and relaxed, see the ball, and let the hands and body do what they have been trained to do.

When preparing to swing the bat, the hitter needs to be sure the shoulders start out level. If the hitter starts the swing with the shoulder in any position other than level,

the bat will follow a poor track to the contact area. The only acceptable shoulder placement other than level is allowing the front shoulder to be slightly tilted downward. The hitter who has a problem with the looping swing track may choose to start with the front shoulder tilted slightly downward to aid in correcting the problem. Quite often, the hitter with a problem lifting the front shoulder will have a loop in the swing. At no time should the front shoulder be lifted to swing. If the front shoulder is lifted, the hitter's head will move. If the eyes move, the hitter will lose sight of the ball. Later, we will go into more detail on the loop or uppercut swing. For the time being, it is important to note an uppercut or loop swing is a swing that allows the track of the bat to start at the bottom of the strike zone and continue up through the strike zone to the contact area. The proper swing has a much more level swing track than the uppercut track.

The front shoulder, as a rule of thumb, should point at the belt buckle of the pitcher on the mound. Shoulders that stray from the belt buckle of the pitcher will make it very difficult for the hitter to cover the strike zone. The shoulders are a very important part of the setup because the shoulders will help the upper body stay in position at the beginning of the swing and help keep the body in a solid position throughout the swing. The upper body will move in the same direction that the shoulders shift, so it is very important that the shoulders stay level and pointed in the right direction at all times.

Starting with the hands, elbows and shoulders in the right position will allow the hitter to spend more time and energy trying to hit the ball hard. The hitter will be making adjustments to the approach during the swing, paying less attention to the swing track and more attention to making the corrections. Hitting a pitched baseball is hard enough; making more work by setting up incorrectly will not help your success rate.

# 2

# Hitting the Ball

# Tracking the Ball

Being able to see the ball, from release to contact, is essential. Learning how to find the ball and when to look for it is a big part of hitting with success.

While standing on deck waiting to get a chance to hit, or when the pitcher is warming up, a hitter needs to watch the pitcher throw the ball. The on-deck area is the area in foul territory, where the next-to-hit hitter is practicing. Be sure to pay special attention to the release point of the pitcher. The release point is the spot where the pitcher releases the ball to the plate. This is important for the hitter because in order to hit the ball a hitter needs to have sight of the ball and its rotation. The sooner the hitter finds the pitched ball, the better able the hitter is to decide if it is a strike. Finding the ball early will also help the hitter figure out whether the pitch is a curveball, slider, split, change, or fastball. Be sure to notice whether the pitcher is releasing the ball from over the head. This is referred to as an overhand release. Beside the head is referred to as high ¾, or the conventional ¾ release. On occasion a pitcher will have a sidearm release, which is when a pitcher releases the

*The hitter should visually find the ball at this point in the pitcher's delivery*

ball far from the side of the body, or underhand, which is referred to as a submarine release. It is to the hitter's advantage to be aware of where the ball will come from when trying to decide if the pitch is a hittable curveball, or straight fastball.

*Overhand release*

*High three-quarters release*

*Low three-quarters release*

Tracking the pitched ball is a big problem, especially for the young hitter. A hitter needs to find the ball early and not lose sight of the ball at any point while it approaches the contact area. The steady-head hitter with good vision will have greater success than the hitter who lets the head move during the swing. The hitter who sets up at the plate with the shoulders rotated too much will look for the ball over the front shoulder. This will cause the hitter to use only one eye to track the ball into the contact area. This hitter will also struggle to find the ball.

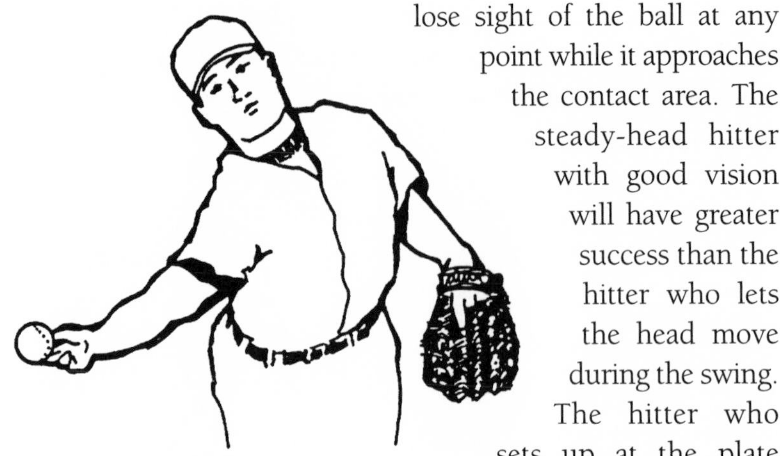

*Sidearm release*

*Submarine release*

## Starting the Swing

Figuring out when to start the swing and how to make contact with the pitch is a problem all hitters have, at every level. There is no way to explain in a book how to have success. We can only give the proper mechanics and hope practice and athletic ability can figure the whole process out. Good hitters have timing and hand-eye coordination. The basic parts of the swing and the proper way to execute the swing can be explained and illustrated, but practice is the only way to create proper timing and hand-eye coordination. Up to this point we have broken down the parts of the swing individually. We will try to put the whole process together. Like anything else, there has to be a start.

## Trigger

Knowing and understanding the reason for the trigger, and using the proper type of trigger, is going to help the hitter get the swing off and running in the right direction.

*Proper hand movement for the trigger*

The trigger is no more than the start of the swing. The trigger is usually the first movement of the hands when the ball is released to the plate by the pitcher. The normal trigger is a movement slightly back from the set position of the hand. Dropping the hands slightly at the release of the pitch is another type of trigger used, but be sure the hands do not make a large move. A large move up or down will result in a hand hitch. We discussed earlier that a hand hitch will cause long swings or poor contact. A short, smooth, direct move with the hands is the most effective trigger. If this type of trigger is used, the hand move comes second. Occasionally, some hitter will use the weight shift and hand move at the same time. The problem with this is that too much is happening at the same time. Try to keep it simple, one move at a time.

The final trigger we will discuss is the slight hip turn. This is not very common, but can be effective. As the pitcher releases the ball or when the hitter decides the swing should start, the hitter's first move is the front hip shifting slightly in the direction of the plate. This will shift the upper body weight and keep the hitter's front side closed. Both of these things are positive for the hitter. This weight shift from the front hip will get the hitter's swing started. Very often this front hip move will come at the same time the hands start back. Be careful not to over-shift the front side. This will cause the body to get in the way of the hands and bat trying to get to the contact area. With all these triggers, be sure that the movement is slow and controlled. A quick move or jerk will cause the hitter's head to move, making it hard to track the ball. The quick move or jerk will also take away the hitter's relaxed, smooth swing, making it hard to make consistent solid contact.

The start of the trigger should be based on the velocity at which the pitcher is throwing, and the quickness the hitter has in the swing. The hitter with a long swing will need to start earlier than the hitter with a short, quick stroke. The pitcher who is throwing very hard will require the hitter to get the bat started earlier, while the off-speed or soft toss pitcher will allow some time for the hitter to get the swing going. There is no formula to tell the hitter when to start the swing. Just make sure the trigger is smooth. Try to stay relaxed and controlled. Do not get anxious and hurry the trigger. Practice and experience are the only ways to get the trigger and timing right.

## Start the Stride

We spoke earlier about the types of strides. Understanding the exact time to get the stride going will allow the hitter to get the swing in position for contact.

The stride should not start before the trigger movement of the hands, but just as the trigger moves. If the stride starts before the hands, the body will be in position to hit while the hands and bat drag to the strike zone. A hitter should use the stride to give the body a chance to transfer the weight to the back leg.

Try to make the stride smooth and easy. A quick jerk or jump to the stride will only allow the head to move, and the head needs to stay steady no matter what. The hands need to work with the stride to create some rhythm. The hitter who allows the trigger and the stride to start separately will have a two-part swing, which will be hard to adjust. As discussed in the hand trigger section, the slight move back for the hands should start just as the hitter lifts the front foot for the stride. The stride needs to be direct to the pitcher's belt buckle. The stride foot should only lift off the ground two to three inches, just enough to move forward freely. The purpose of the stride is to transfer the weight of the upper body from centered between the legs to the back leg, which is then referred to as loaded. The weight needs to be set on the back leg, so the hitter can stay behind the ball and create power.

## Bat Track

Getting everything started is very important; getting the swing in the proper position for contact is even more important. Having the body in position to swing is great, but the bat needs to be in the right position in order to hit the ball. The bat track is the key to getting the bat to the contact area correctly.

The swing or bat track is the direction that the bat travels from the start of the swing to the finish. The swing is not finished at contact. The finish of the swing occurs when the body stops the bat after extension. The swing track begins behind the hitter when the bat is loaded in the hands, ready for the pitch. When the trigger starts, the bat track is started. The bat and hands should start back slightly in the

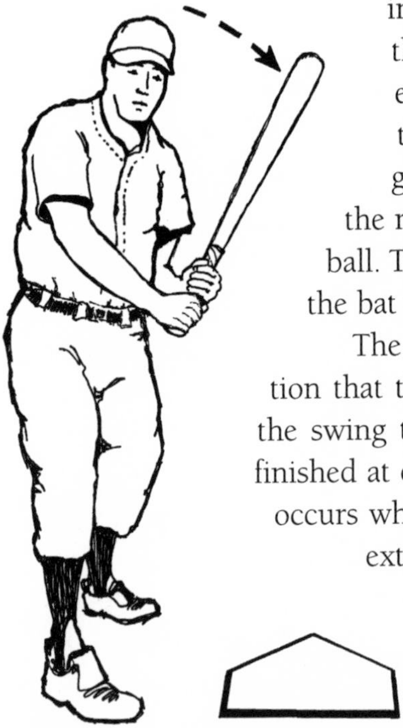

*Starting the swing down into the strike zone*

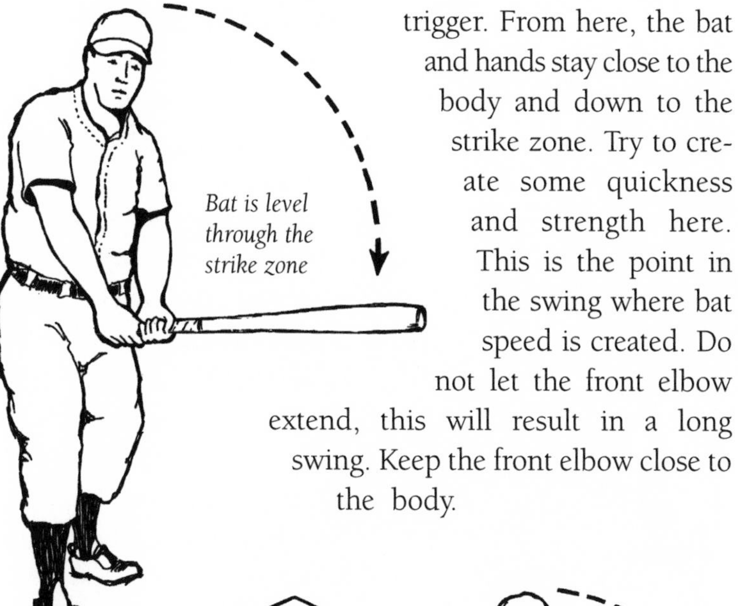


trigger. From here, the bat and hands stay close to the body and down to the strike zone. Try to create some quickness and strength here. This is the point in the swing where bat speed is created. Do not let the front elbow extend, this will result in a long swing. Keep the front elbow close to the body.

Try not to muscle up, stay relaxed and loose. A proper bat track will throw the hands to the strike zone. During the hand-throwing process the knob of the bat should be driven to the plate. This will allow for the hands to drive down to the strike zone. The barrel of the bat should not be first to get to the strike zone. The knob should reach the strike zone first. As the knob

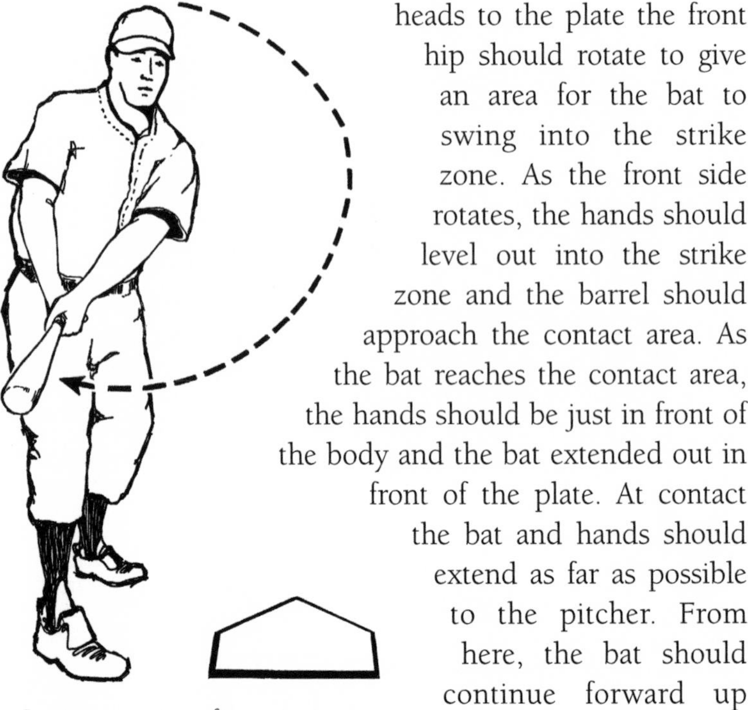

*Continue swinging after contact is made*

heads to the plate the front hip should rotate to give an area for the bat to swing into the strike zone. As the front side rotates, the hands should level out into the strike zone and the barrel should approach the contact area. As the bat reaches the contact area, the hands should be just in front of the body and the bat extended out in front of the plate. At contact the bat and hands should extend as far as possible to the pitcher. From here, the bat should continue forward up over the front shoulder to the area next to the hitter's neck. Very often the bat will stop when it hits the hitter's back.

It is important to remember that the bat should not slow down throughout the swing, even after contact. Let the bat travel in a natural motion, uninterrupted by the contact with the hit ball. A bat stopped at contact is referred to as "cutting off the swing." This will result in loss of power and a lack of control of the swing.

A hitter's track is normally based on the hitter's mechanics. Sometimes a hitter can move the bat during the swing to purposely make a correction, but usually, the hitter's bat track is created by mechanics and strength the hitter provides. The bat track can be affected by the stance, hand position, bottom-half mechanics, or placement of the pitch in the strike zone. The ideal bat track is direct and quick through the strike zone with a limited amount of effort, but generating the most amount of bat speed. The bat track should never cause the hitter to lose balance or lose sight of the pitch.

We will spend a lot of time explaining the mechanics to develop the proper swing and the way to strike the ball correctly, but not much time discussing the bat track. The reason for this is that a proper swing and good mechanics will develop the desired bat track naturally. Mechanics will make or break the proper bat track. The effective hitter will develop solid mechanics.

## Contact Area

The contact area is the area out in front of the plate where the ball is to be hit by the bat. This area is identical to the strike zone but six to ten inches out in front of the plate. A hitter needs to decide if the pitched ball is a strike, and beat the ball to the plate with the bat hitting the pitch before it travels into the strike zone. The ideal swing will allow the hitter to make contact at full extension in the contact area, as opposed to making contact over the plate. A pitch that is allowed to get to the plate before contact is much harder to hit in fair territory than the pitch hit in front of the plate.

## Bottom Half Position in Swing

During the swing the arms are busy trying to get the bat into the contact area. During this process it is important that the body also gets into a hitting position. As discussed earlier, the body weight should be firm on the back leg at the start of the swing. As the swing starts and the knob of the bat is heading to the plate, the front foot should reach the ground, completing the stride. From here, the front hip should rotate slightly to the plate just as the front shoulder should. This movement will allow the hitter to cock the upper body while still resting the majority of the body weight on the back knee. Sometimes a hitter will cock the upper body just before the front stride foot reaches the ground. This is fine as long as the move is smooth and a hitter can keep the weight on the back leg. The front leg

*Proper hip rotation to start the swing*

should now firm up to allow the back leg to pivot and throw the weight forward. With a firm front leg, a brace is developed. As the bat reaches the contact area, this brace will allow the hitter to develop lower body power in the swing. If a hitter is not braced at contact, the ball will vibrate the hitter and cause power to be lost. The stride foot is planted to the ground with the front foot slightly closed. (By closed we mean the front foot should be pointed to the plate and not the pitcher.) As the hips and front shoulder rotate, with the bat in the contact area, the back foot should pivot on the ball of the foot. This is sometimes called "smooshing the bug," because it is much like the action a

*Make contact with the ball in front of the plate*

*The "Power L"*

person would make when stepping on a bug on the floor. The right-handed hitter should rotate the back foot in a counterclockwise fashion, remembering to keep the ball of the foot in contact with the ground. As the back foot rotates to hit the ball, the knee should stay bent at a 90-degree angle. If looking at the back leg in this position, the leg should be in the shape of an L. This angle is often referred to as the "power L." This will keep flexibility in the bottom half of the body for the hitter in the swing. A stiff back leg will often cause the hitter to hit the ball with the back foot off the ground. A back foot off the ground will decrease the power a hitter can generate. As the hitter rotates on the back leg, the weight of the upper body should rest on the back

*Keep a firm front leg but also keep the body centered between both feet—don't lunge at the ball, but stay balanced*

hip with the body centered between the two legs. The weight should not rest on the front side of the body. Hitters that let the weight fall forward in the swing will struggle staying back on the pitch. This hitter will lunge at pitches, instead of using the hands and balance to make solid contact. This hitter is referred to as a "front foot hitter" and will not have power to drive balls. The upper body in a perfect swing is exactly in the middle of both legs, just as it was at the beginning of the stance.

## Balance

Balance is one of the most important elements of hitting. Without balance, a hitter will not be able to track the ball effectively and no power can be developed. Proper balance allows the hitter to stay in control throughout the entire swing, making solid contact possible. To create balance, first center the upper body over the legs. As we discussed earlier, the upper body should be centered over the feet in the stance. Gain the proper grip and set the bat in the proper position, ready to make contact with the pitched ball. At this point, with the upper body centered between the legs, the weight of the upper body needs to shift slightly to the back leg. The back leg will provide power. (If the weight is placed primarily on the front leg, the hitter will find it hard to stay back and wait for the pitch.) This shift of the body weight is called "setting the weight." With a centered upper body, the legs do not have to do extra work during the swing to regain balance. As the hitter starts to swing the bat, the upper weight should be entirely moved to the back leg while the front foot strides.

The back leg, with the upper body weight on it, along with the back hip, should carry the weight through the swing. This weight shift should cause the back leg to hold the body until the front foot returns to the ground, to be used as a brace for the lower body. When the front foot is braced, the back leg should throw the weight forward in a rotating action. This will create power for the swing. This rotation will also make room for the swing to happen.

If a hitter leaves the weight of the body forward in the stance during the stride, the front foot will not be able to brace. If the front foot does not brace, the velocity of the ball will cause a loss of power at contact. The strength of the upper body is not prepared to take on the force of the pitched ball. A hitter may be able to hit the ball solid and get a line drive, but the power hit will not occur when the weight is too far forward during the swing.

A hitter that starts the weight totally over the back leg will often have a spin-type swing. This means instead of working the stride and swinging the bat properly, the hitter will find the body spinning towards the foul line too early, allowing the head and front shoulder to fall off the pitch. The right-handed hitter will spin towards the third base line, and the left-handed hitter will fall toward the first base line. The spin-type hitter will look fine early in the swing, but will fall off to the base lines just as the ball reaches the contact area. If the lower body is shifted correctly, the swing should be balanced from the start to the middle of the swing where the bat reaches the plate.

From here, the front shoulder becomes the issue. If the hitter can keep the front shoulder pointed at the pitcher from the start of the swing to the point where contact is to be made, balance has most likely been achieved. The hitter that lets the front shoulder move early in the swing will allow the balance to fall off the pitch. The front shoulder should not move, but if any movement is made it should be toward the plate. Any shoulder movement to the base lines will cause the hitter's head to pull of the ball and weight to leave center. The shoulders control the upper body. Try to keep the upper body on top of the legs during the swing.

One other weight-control aid is to keep the weight on the balls of the feet. Do not let the weight of the upper body fall onto the heels. A good hitter keeps the balance on the balls of the feet, just as in any other sport. Flat-footed hitters will not be able to make adjustments.

Because of the way a swing is developed, the bottom hand will remain on the bat throughout the extension. Make sure to keep a good grip with the bottom hand. Losing the bat at extension will result in a loss of the power developed throughout the swing. The top hand will release the bat just as the bat reaches full extension out in front of the plate. This extension will allow the hitter to finish the rotation of the upper body and the completion of the hands through the ball. The extension portion of the swing is very important because the hitter is completing the swing track that has been the main focus of the swing from the start. To cut off the swing out in front of the plate before extension will defeat the hard work and effort put in to developing a good swing. The bat speed developed in the swing can easily be wasted if the extension is shortened. Let the bat fly to the finish and drive the ball.

## Extension

After contact the hitter has only finished half the swing. The finish of the swing is made up of the extension out in front of the plate. Getting the bat to finish the swing is important for many reasons, the most important of which is power. A swing that does not get extension will never develop the power a hitter needs to be successful.

A hitter should strive for the bat to be fully extended at contact. A hitter with good extension at contact also has the front elbow fully extended to the straight position out in front of the plate. If the hitter can get the front arm locked to full extension and the bat extended out in front of the plate, all that is left is for the ball to be hit on the sweet spot of the bat.

Be sure not to extend the front arm too early. The front arm should never be extended except out in front of the plate. Throughout the swing the front arm should be slightly bent at the elbow. This will allow for a quick swing and ability to make adjustments on the pitched ball. As the bat is thrown into the strike zone with the aid of the back arm, the front arm will extend fully.

*Proper front elbow extension at contact*

## Contact

The swing is designed to hit the ball on the sweet spot of the bat. As discussed earlier the sweet spot is out on the barrel of the bat. This is the point of the bat where the best hits are made. The hitter should build the mechanics and

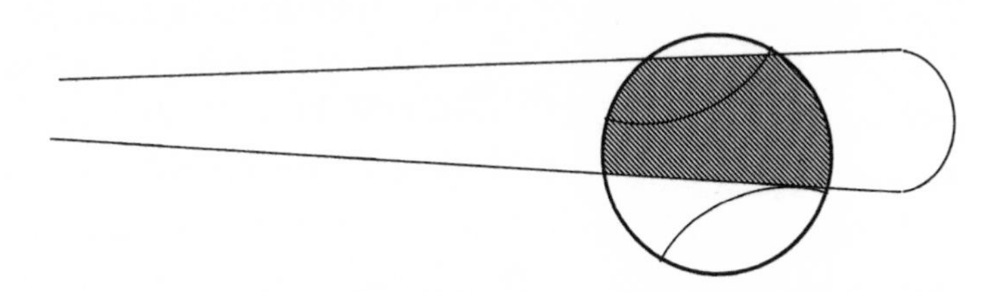

*Hit the top half of the ball*

swing track to best get the barrel to the contact area to make solid contact. The hitter should attempt to find the ball as it is released from the pitcher to the plate. As the ball reaches the contact area and the hitter decides the pitched ball is a hittable pitch, the hitter needs to perform the swing to make contact.

The ball needs to be struck on the upper half of the ball. A hitter who tries to hit the ball on the bottom half of the ball will often pop the ball up. The upper half of the ball is better because the proper swing brings the bat to contact in a slightly downward angle. The downward plane of the swing allows the hitter, who is using a round bat, to make better contact with the upper half of the ball than the bottom. The downward swing will naturally put backspin on the ball when it is struck. If a hitter hits the ball on the ground, the defense will have to catch the ground ball and make an accurate throw to complete the out. The ball hit on the bottom half of the ball or just below center will leave the ball in the air, requiring the defense only to catch the ball to finish the out. There is a much better chance to reach base if the ball is struck on the ground rather than in the air. The ball hit with backspin that stays in the air after leaving the bat will carry much father than the ball hit on the bottom half. The backspin given to the ball on the slight downward swing will cut through the air and carry well.

## Hand Control

In connection with balance, the hitter needs to keep the hands under control. This is much easier said than done. A hitter needs to make sure the hands swing the bat, but at the same time not allow the hands and bat to get to the contact area too early. As the body shifts to hit the ball, a hitter needs to be careful not to rush the swing. If the pitcher changes the speed on the pitch, the hitter needs to keep the hands in a position to make a swing even if the body has been fooled by the pitch. Although the perfect swing brings the bat and body into the contact area together, the hands can still hit with some degree of success by themselves. The hitter needs to make the adjustments with the hands. Relax, stay back and hit the ball with the hands. The velocity of the pitch will provide enough power to let the hands be effective. A good hitter can see the pitch early, notice the need for an adjustment and move to keep the hands in position to hit the ball. The hitter needs to throw the hands in the direction of the pitch. Do not throw the hands to where the ball is at the start of the swing. Read the pitch, decide where it will finish, and meet the ball there with the hands. If a hitter can detect the type of pitch and the speed of the pitch, adjust the hands and put a good swing on the ball.

## Position Points

These are a few points to keep in mind when setting up in the batter's box, preparing to hit. When the feet are set in the stance the knees should be facing the plate. The hitter who does not square up to the plate will struggle getting solid body position in the swing. The hitter should also pay attention that the upper body is square to the plate. To check this, make sure the belt buckle is pointed directly at the plate, not forward or behind it. Otherwise, the body will be too open or too closed. Too open happens when the buckle is forward of the plate, too closed means the buckle is pointed behind the plate. If the buckle is behind the plate, the upper body is over-rotated and it is very difficult to rotate the body to the strike zone in time to get a good swing. As the swing is produced the belt buckle will rotate from facing the plate to facing the pitcher at the end of the swing. This move with the belt buckle will ensure that the upper body rotated correctly.

## Head Placement

As mentioned before, locating the pitched ball as soon as possible is a must. The eyes need to find the ball quickly and never lost sight of the pitch while in flight to the plate. In order to do this the head needs to be steady. A hitter who has a swing that causes the head to move will have a tough time keeping sight of the pitched ball. The head needs to stay level, facing the pitcher and in a position where both eyes can see the ball the entire time, from pitcher's motion to contact with the bat. Very often the hitter will tilt the head to a position where only one eye can locate the ball. A head in proper position will find the chin resting against the front shoulder at the beginning of the swing, and resting against the back shoul-

*Improper head angle (head tilt)*

der at the finish. The head does not move during the swing. Instead, the upper body rotates, shifting the shoulders and changing the relative position of the chin. The head should be behind the swing as contact is made, not over the contact area, or ahead of contact. A proper swing will allow the head to stay over the back knee and see the ball out in front of the plate with the bat making contact.

## The Knees

Even though the knees face the plate at the start of the stance, they will finish facing the pitcher. With the proper back foot rotation as described earlier, the back knee should rotate to face the pitcher. This will aid in the rotation of the upper body. Be sure that the back foot never leaves the ground during the back knee rotation. The front knee will rotate to face the pitcher because of the force developed by the upper body rotation during the swing. The front knee will not face the pitcher until after contact has been made. The

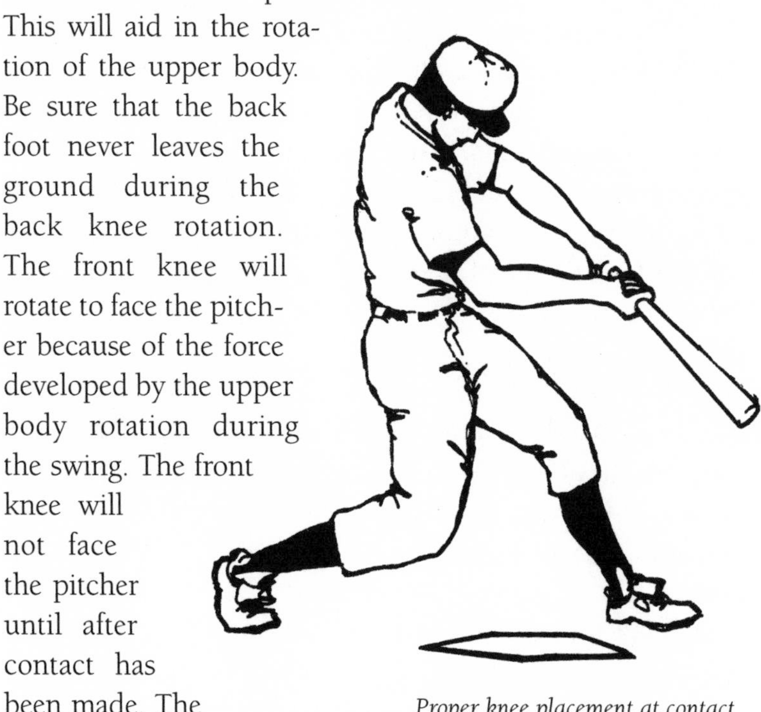

*Proper knee placement at contact*

front knee will remain facing the plate until the bat head extends out in front of the plate.

A knee that rotates too early will allow the hitter to fall off the swing and lose balance. A well-planted front leg and rotation of the backside will make this knee shift natural and easy. A front foot that leaves the ground or strides in the wrong direction will make the front knee placement impossible. When practicing your swings, before stepping into the batter's box, pay special attention to how the knees work. The bottom half movement cannot be done successfully without proper knee shift.

## Swing Types

There are three basic types of swings. These swings can be by design, but most often the swing is natural to the hitter. Some hitters have the ability to hit home runs and have power. Some hitters put the ball in play, and run the bases. Some hitters can put both types of hits together, and hit for average and power. Although size and strength have a lot to do with what type of hitter you are, the type of swing also plays a part.

### LINE DRIVE SWING

The line drive hitter usually hits at the top of the order and has the ability to line the ball into the gaps and run the bases. This swing is developed in the swing track. A line drive hitter will let the hands do most of the work in the swing. The hands will stay above the ball all the way into the contact area. The swing will have a slightly downward plane as contact is made. The line drive swing is very short and compact. This swing develops no lift and the hitter attempts to hit the outside pitch into the opposite field and the inside pitch to the pull field. Many hits by the line drive hitter are low to the ground and up the middle. Balance is important, but the body does not provide a lot of power. Often a line drive hitter will find contact made with the weight too far forward in the swing. Line drive hitters will seldom strike out. Usually, this hitter has average body size.

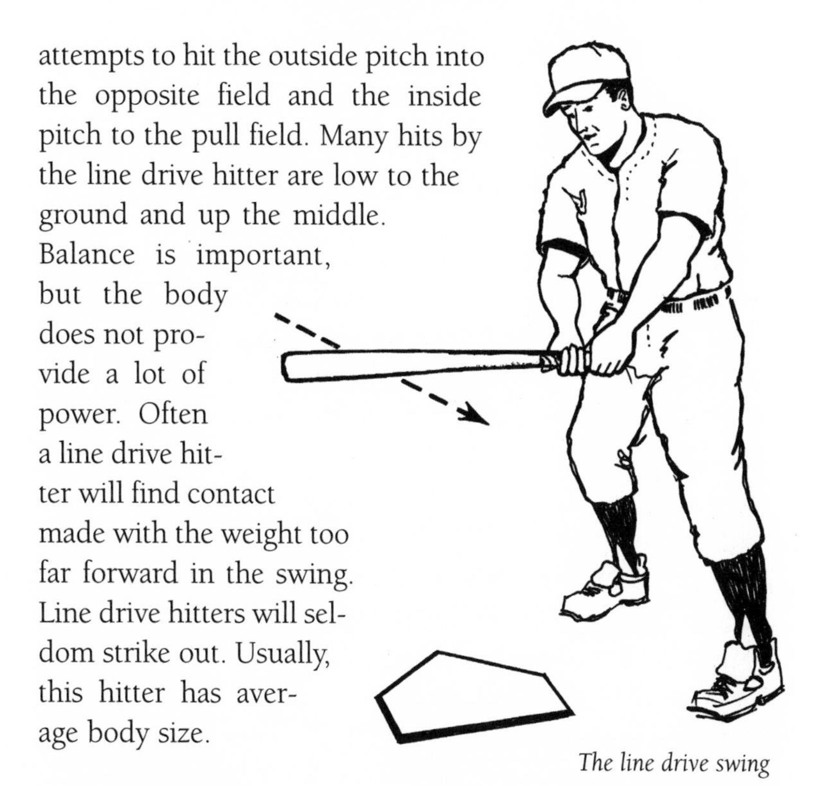

*The line drive swing*

## LOFT SWING

The loft-type swinger is normally a home run or power hitter. Most often this type of loft swing is a strong, large player. The loft hitter will most often put the ball in the air at contact and fly out often. The loft hitter will strike out more than most hitters, because the swing does not allow for the hitter to make many adjustments after the bat starts the swing. The loft hitter is attempting to put the ball in the outfield with a long uppercut swing track.

A large amount of hand movement in the trigger is common in the loft swing. The loft swing is developed when the hitter drops the hands during the trigger.

Dropping the hands in the trigger will cause the bat to make an uppercut track to the contact area. Because of the uppercut angle on the swing, contact will often be made on the bottom half of the ball. The loft hitter will keep the weight on the back hip throughout the swing. Collapsing on the back knee is a common problem for these hitters. Another very common problem for the loft swinger is pulling off the ball. A loft hitter tries to pull the ball, so over-rotating the hips and shoulders causes pulling off the pitch. The loft hitter will hit in the middle of the order and drive in a majority of the team's runs. A loft type hitter who does not have the strength to hit the ball over the fence is a poor hitter with a low average.

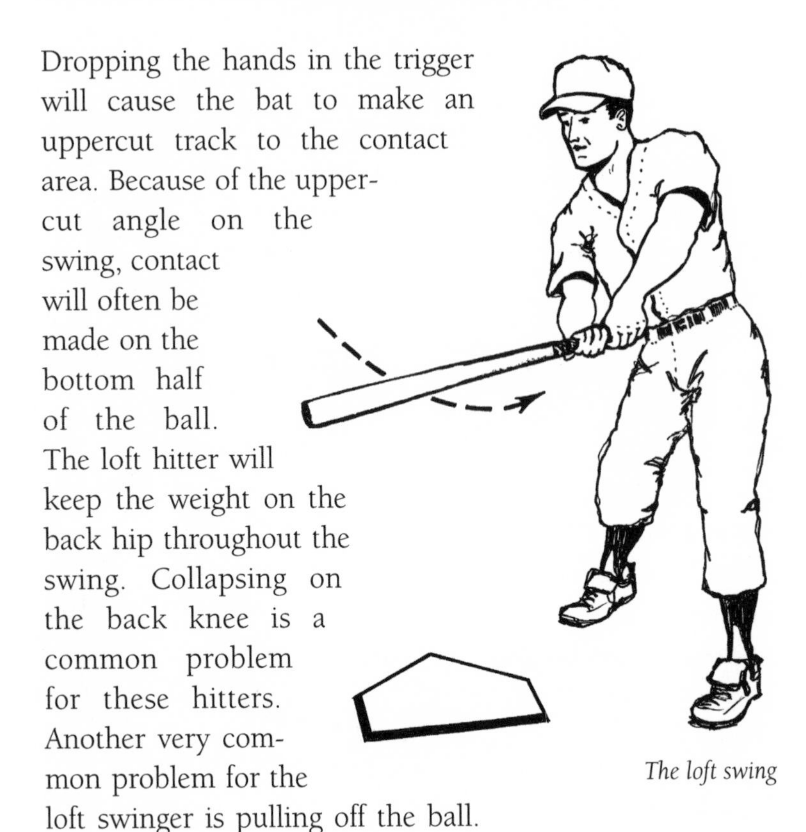

*The loft swing*

## SLAP SWING

The slap hitter will be the hitter scoring the run. The slap hitter's job is to get on base and score runs. The slap hitter is most often a speed type player and bats at the top of the order. This type of hitter is expected to get on base. A slap hitter may also hit at the bottom of the order to get on base for the upper half of the order, which follows. The slap hitter seldom strikes out. The slap hitter has a very short swing with relatively little power. The slap hitter gets very little power out of the legs and hips.

Hand-eye coordination is most important for the slap hitter. The important point for this hitter is to keep the hands back and make contact with a chopping swing. Starting the hands very close to the strike zone and making a very short swing is the aim. A downward type swing track is very important for the slap hitter. This hitter is trying to make contact with the top of the ball and hit ground balls. Unlike the other types of hitters, the slap hitter may let the ball get to the plate before contact. This type of hitter is also known to bunt for a base hit.

*The slap swing*

# 3

# Reading Pitches

It may seem that there is no place for pitching in a hitting book, but in order to be a successful hitter, knowing what a pitcher is doing is to a hitter's advantage. When the hitter gets into the batter's box, the pitcher and hitter are in a battle. To know what the pitcher is trying to do and have a basic working knowledge of the pitcher's plan give the hitter an edge. Knowing how to read pitches and what locations are most likely to be used in the count can greatly improve the hitter's chances. Tracking the pitch has been discussed, but to be able to detect different pitches early will allow the hitter to make adjustments early and easily.

The first order of business after setting up in the stance is to find the ball. Tracking the ball is a vital part of a successful swing. As the pitcher releases the ball, the hitter first needs to determine the velocity at which the ball is traveling. If the ball is fast, the pitch is a fastball. If the ball is slow, it is a changeup. The start of the stride and swing are determined by the speed of the pitch. The fastball requires the start of the swing earlier than the changeup. After deciding velocity, rotation of the ball is important. We will now discuss the different types of pitches and rotations. We will explain what a pitcher needs to do to produce rotation on the ball.

## Fastball

The fastball requires the pitcher to keep his hand behind the ball at release. The ball will have backspin as it approaches the plate. This pitch will normally be straight. If the pitcher's hand is not directly behind the ball at release, it may have some run. Run on the fastball means it will move from side to side as it travels to the plate. A right-handed pitcher will make the ball release over the middle of the plate, and come back to the inside corner for the right-handed hitter. The left-handed pitcher releasing the ball over the middle of the plate will make the ball go away to the outside corner of the plate when throwing to a right-handed hitter. A pitcher throwing a pitch with the overhand or high three-fourths release point will usually have this type of action on the fast ball. The pitcher that releases the ball with a three-fourths or low three-fourths release will make the ball sink when it reaches the plate. This sink is the result of the hand coming off the inside of the ball, giving the side-to-side rotation required to make the ball sink. Along with the sink the ball will have some degree of run, much like the overhand or high three-fourths thrower. The sidearm or underhand pitcher will always have sink. This sink is the sole reason for a pitcher to throw from the underhand position.

*The fastball release*

The main concern for the hitter with a fastball is velocity. The ball may run or sink some, but the hitter needs to be sure the bat gets to the contact area in time to make contact with the pitch. The movement on the fastball may affect the hitter's contact, but the velocity of the pitch is a bigger factor to the hitter.

## Curveball

The curveball will have a slower speed than a fastball. It is not uncommon for a curveball to travel 10–15 miles-per-hour slower than the fastball. Along with change of speed, the curveball will also have movement much different than that of the fastball. A curveball will be released with overspin, instead of the backspin of a fastball. As the pitcher releases the ball, the fingers will come off the front of the ball, instead of staying behind the ball as with the fastball. This overspin will cause the ball to travel down to the plate with a rolling, sweeping action. The over spin

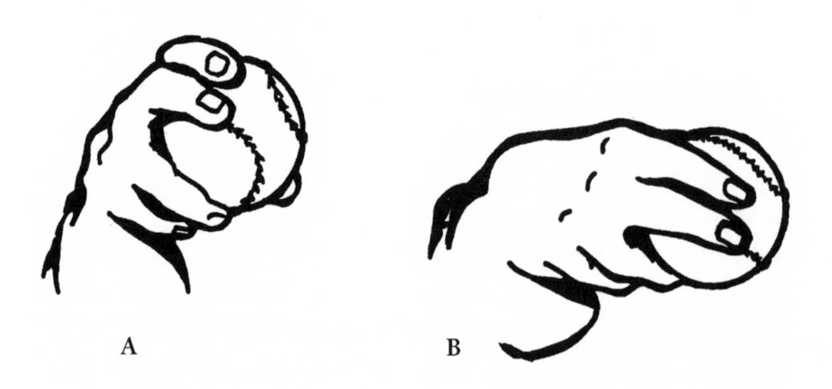


*Curveball wrist action (right-handed pitcher)*

makes the curveball start at the release point and break downward to the hitter. The majority of the downward action will occur within five feet of the plate. As the overhand pitcher releases the curveball, the ball will sweep away from the right-handed hitter in addition to the sink discussed. The three-fourths type pitcher will have sweep to the curveball with less downward movement. This action will be longer than the down type discussed with the overhand pitcher. The sidearm pitcher will make the curveball sweep to the plate. The sidearm curveball will have long action. A right-handed pitcher will release the curveball behind the right-handed hitter's back and curve the ball back to the plate. The underhand pitcher will also sweep the curveball to the plate, occasionally making the ball rise as it sweeps to the plate because the fingers are below the ball as it comes out of the pitcher's hand.

As a hitter, the rotation you see on the ball will tip you off to the pitch. Another thing to look for when trying to detect a curveball is change in the plane of the ball. As the pitcher releases the curveball, the ball will travel up slightly at release. A fastball will come out of the pitcher's hand and head to the plate with no change in plane. The curveball will roll out of the pitcher's hand differently than a fastball, changing the plane the ball travels. Watch the release point and look for this plane change.

## Slider

This pitch usually comes from a hard thrower. The pitcher with an average or slower fastball cannot get the rotation needed to throw a slider properly. The slider is thrown with rotation much like a football. The slider will

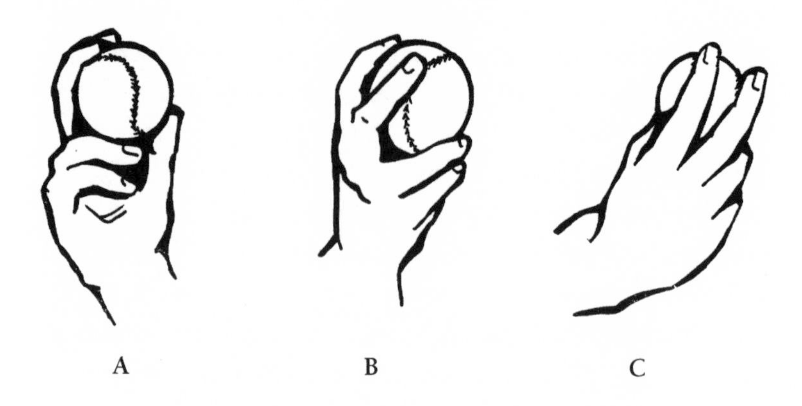


*Sequence of the slider wrist action (right-handed pitcher)*

*Telltale sign of a slider, as the hitter sees it: a red dot appears on the ball in the lower right (from a right-handed pitcher) or lower left (from a left-handed pitcher)*

have rotation causing the ball to have a side-to-side action like a curveball, but with more velocity. The pitcher will release the slider with the fingers on the side of the ball. The ball will rotate very quickly, often causing the ball to form a red dot on the bottom portion of the ball. This dot is a result of the ball rotating so quickly that the seams appear to blend together. A hitter can see this dot as the ball gets halfway from the mound to the plate. Unlike the curveball, the slider will look like a fastball. The action on a good slider is late, just as it approaches the plate. The slider will only work if it is down in the strike zone. A slider that is pitched up in the strike zone will be very easy to hit. A hitter needs to see the dot on the ball and stay back to hit this pitch successfully.

## Knuckleball

This pitch is very uncommon. Very few pitchers can throw this pitch. The ones that do throw the knuckleball cannot throw it over the plate. The knuckleball has no rotation as it travels to the plate. Ball movement is unpredictable. This pitch will have a floating action, up and down all on the same throw. The pitch is thrown very slow and has as few as zero rotations on it as it travels from the release point to the plate.

*Knuckleball grip*

The hitter needs to stay relaxed and patient. Let the ball travel a great distance before starting the swing. The speed of the pitch makes it hard to stay balanced, but the good knuckleball makes it very hard to predict where and what the movement may be. The hitter needs to watch the release point as always. The knuckleball pitcher will shove the ball to the plate, not throw the ball as usual. The fingers will be high off the top of the ball at release. This will also help the hitter detect the pitch.

## Split Finger (Forkball)

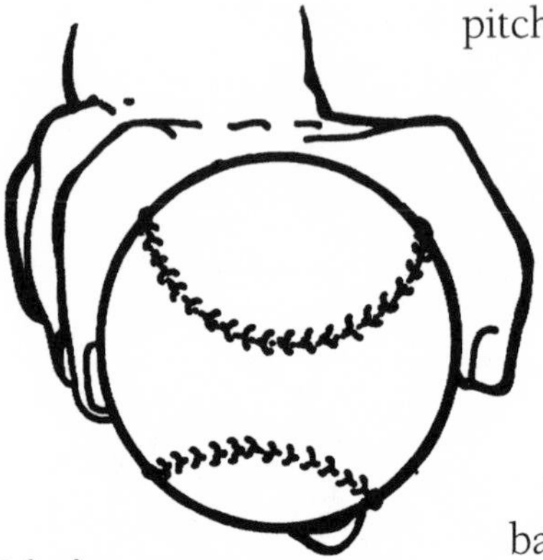

The split finger pitch is most commonly used by the hard thrower. The pitcher who does not have a good fastball will find the split finger grip only flips the ball to the plate, making it easy to see and easy to hit. This pitch will travel to the plate like a fastball, and then drop as it gets to the contact area. The ball will have backspin like a fastball, but with less rotation than a fastball. A hitter may be able to detect the pitch by lack of rotation, but very often the lack of rotation is seen too late to make the adjustments. The pitcher will release the pitch with the fingers split far apart. The ball will be jammed between the two throwing fingers. This may be detected by the hitter at release, but very often is disguised well by the pitcher. The split will be most effective low out of the strike zone. This pitch will start out a strike and drop out of the strike zone at the contact area. The split finger pitch thrown up in the strike zone will look like a poor fastball and often be hit hard, because the ball will straighten out and stay up in the strike zone.

*Split-finger grip*

As a hitter, try to be selective. Stay back and do not chase the split that falls out of the strike zone. A hitter needs to set up at the plate, ready to hit the fastball. Do not set up and try to guess what pitch is coming. Prepare for the fastball and make adjustments as the other pitches are thrown. A hitter that can detect the off-speed pitches as they are released will be very successful, but looking for and swinging at strikes is the best plan. Do not let the pitcher throw pitches out of the strike zone and get you to chase them.

## Pitch Location

To this point, we have focused all out attention on mechanics. When hitting the pitched ball, mechanics are

*Three zones for pitch location*

very important. Getting the body in the proper position to enable a hitter to put the ball in play with power and leverage takes many hours of practice. Another part of hitting correctly is knowing what to do with the pitch when it approaches the contact area. We will now discuss the best way to hit pitches located in different sections of the plate and at different points in the count. Before we start, we need to first divide the strike zone into sections.

The beginner should break the strike zone into three different areas. The inside six inches, middle six inches, and the outside six inches will be a good starting point for the young hitter. No matter where the pitch is in the zone, it is still important to work the mechanics and make solid contact. We will explain these zones and what the hitter should try to do, not what they have to do.

## THE INSIDE PITCH

When the pitched ball is on the inside portion of the plate, the hitter should try to hit the ball to the pull field—the field behind the front shoulder of the hitter. The right-handed hitter's pull field is left field; the left-handed hitter's pull field is right field. The ball on the inside third of the plate is the easiest to hit to the pull field, The hitter should attempt to make contact with the pitch out in front of the plate, in the contact area, at the point where extension starts in the swing. When a proper swing is executed, the ball will naturally travel to the pull field. If a hitter tries to hit the inside pitch to the opposite field it is referred to as "inside-outing" the pitch. The proper swing will allow the hitter to drive the ball when hit correctly. When the hitter inside-outs the pitch, the hitter will keep the hands too close to the body and the body will interrupt the proper swing. The inside-out swing is used when trying to advance the runner in a hit-and-run play, or when the hitter is fooled by the pitch. Generally speaking, the hitter should not attempt to inside-out the pitch.

Occasionally, the hitter may be able to make the proper swing and drive the pitch to center field. In this case the hitter is able to keep the hands in and out in front of the body with the bat level at contact, causing the ball to travel up the middle. The hitter will have limited power to center field on this pitch, but getting a hit is just as important. The important points when hitting the inside pitch are getting out in front of the pitch and getting extension.

## THE OUTSIDE PITCH

For most pitches we try to hit the ball out in front of the plate. On the outside pitch, however, the hitter should let the ball get to just to the front edge of the plate before making contact. The pitch on the outer section of the plate needs to be hit to the opposite field, the field facing the hitter. The right-handed hitter will hit the ball to right field; the left-handed hitter will hit the ball to left field.

Patience is important on an outside pitch. The anxious hitter will try to start the swing early and jump at the ball, which will result in a ground ball or a swing-and-miss. The loop swing will be an infield pop up. The hitter with the proper approach to the outside pitch will wait a fraction of a second longer and let the ball get deep into the contact area. The outside pitch is naturally far from the body, so the hitter cannot keep the hands close to the body unless the pitch is deep in the contact area. Allowing the ball to get further to the plate will allow the hitter to keep the hands nearer the body during the swing. The hitter trying to hit the outside pitch out in the front of the plate will overextend the hands and cause the swing to get too long. If you allow the outside pitch to get to the front of the plate, and hit it to the opposite field, the ball will be at its closest point when you make contact. The outside pitch can be driven to center field if the hitter allows the ball to get too deep in the contact area, and gets the hands out in front of the body, just as on the inside pitch. Most power hitters that have success with the outside pitch will drive the ball to the opposite field gap. The power hitter will have more trouble with this pitch, because the swing is usually long and the pull field is their goal.

## THE PITCH DOWN THE MIDDLE

The pitch down the middle is the most hittable of all the locations in the strike zone. Unlike the ball on the outside portion of the plate, or the ball on the inside, the middle takes the least amount of effort to make solid contact. The pitch located in the middle of the plate can be hit in a few different areas of the field. The ball away is struck just in front of the plate, the inside pitch is hit six inches out in front of the plate. The pitch down the middle can be hit in either area. The pitch down the middle hit out in front of the plate is driven to the pull field, while the middle pitch hit just off the front of the plate will be driven to the center field. The ball hit just as it gets to the plate will be driven into the opposite field. Because the middle pitch can be hit in all of these areas, it means the ball down the middle is very hittable, so all pitchers are taught to stay away from the middle of the plate. A hitter needs to make sure, just as with any other pitch, to stay balanced and try to hit the ball with solid mechanics. Just because the ball is thrown down the middle does not mean over-swing or get anxious. Hit this pitch based on the situation in the game and what the team needs.

## THE HIGH PITCH

It is easier to hit the ball up in the strike zone than the ball down. The reason for this is that the high pitch, up in

*High and low pitch zones*

the strike zone, is closer to the hitter's eyes and thus easier for the hitter to see and decide where it needs to be hit. The hard thrower will have more success up in the strike zone than the slow thrower. This is because the high pitch is above the hands, and the hitter will have trouble getting the hands up to the fastball in time to make a good swing. The off-speed pitch, up in the zone, is usually flat and slow making it very hittable. Be careful not to chase the high pitch out of the strike zone. Make sure the pitch is still a strike. Keep the swing under control and focus on hitting the middle or upper half of the ball. This is called staying on top of the ball. To do this, get the hands above the ball in the swing. The hands that stay below the ball will cause a loop or uppercut swing, both of which will cause a fly ball or pop up. Remember to keep the hands high and stay balanced. Drive the ball based on the area of the plate where the ball is located.

## THE LOW PITCH

The low pitch is the preferred pitch for the pitcher. A pitcher that can keep the ball down in the strike zone will be most effective. The low pitch is difficult for the hitter to lift in the air and is farthest from the hitter's eyes, making it hardest for the hitter to get a good look at and make solid contact. The low pitch is normally struck on the top of the ball, making a ground ball common.

In order for the hitter to hit this pitch hard, or in the air, the hitter needs to find a way to get to the center of the ball. The proper swing on the low pitch is to keep the head steady, drive down through the ball and finish the swing with extension. The most effective low pitch hitter will hit the ball where it is pitched. For instance, if the pitched ball is low and away, drive that pitch to the opposite field. Make a swing with the hands on top of the ball, and the downward plane will allow the hitter to drive the ball hard on the ground or in a low line drive. The swing that is looped or long will play right into the pitcher's hands. These types of swings will produce pop ups or soft fly balls, easy outs for the defense.

If possible, having some flexibility in the knees is helpful for the hitter attempting to make a swing at the low pitch. This flexibility will allow the hitter to get a better angle to the ball, and a lower body position. Do not overswing. A solid, mechanically sound swing is the proper approach.

## Important Check Points

It is easy to talk about the "perfect swing, " but very hard to make it happen. There are many parts to a swing and keeping track of the parts is hard. The following list is a guide to where the parts should be during the swing. Getting most of the parts in position to hit is probably enough to have success.

**1.** At the beginning of the swing, be sure the feet are firm on the ground in the stance. If the feet are not planted on the ground a firm base is not established. It is very important to have a firm base, or balance will not be achieved. With the feet firm on the ground it is much easier to stay still without body movement prior to the pitch.

**2.** Be comfortable with the width of the stance. If a hitter cannot get comfortable in the box, full attention cannot be given to the pitched ball. You need to focus on the ball without distractions.

**3.** Be sure the distance between your stance and the plate will allow for proper plate coverage. So often a hitter will set up in the box too far from the plate. Give yourself a chance to hit—don't set up the plate in a position where failure is easy.

**4.** Set your hands in a comfortable spot while getting prepared to pick up the pitched ball. Hands that start in the wrong position will cause the hitter to struggle getting the bat into the proper swing track for solid contact. It does not take much for the track to get too long or be at the wrong angle.

**5.** Along with the hands position, a hitter should check the angle of the bat in the set position. Just a slight tilt of the bat in the wrong direction will cause the swing to get long or get in the wrong angle, much like the wrong hand position. A bat in the wrong angle often will cause poor plate coverage.

**6.** It is a must that throughout the swing a hitter stays balanced. If a hitter loses proper balance, hitting becomes almost impossible. Balance is the most important part of a good swing. Balance affects your ability to see the ball, control of the body, speed of the swing, and contact.

**7.** Be sure to get the stride foot back to the ground in time for contact. Often a hitter will get caught with the front foot still in the air at contact. This will affect balance and strength. A hitter who can get the front foot back to the ground will allow for adjustments throughout the swing.

**8.** Have slow feet during the swing. Anxious, quick-moving feet will cause a smooth flowing swing to be lost. Remind yourself as you set up, "slow feet and quick hands."

**9.** Just as the feet need to be slow, once in place they need to stay there. Any extra movement with the feet during the stride will cause the body to get set to hit late. When trying to get in position to hit, keeping your feet under control is a must.

**10.** Be sure to get to the contact area at the proper time. Do not let the ball get over the plate. Any pitched ball that gets to the plate without contact will have traveled too far for the hitter to get a proper swing. The pitched ball has to be hit out in front of the plate. As soon as you decide that the ball is a strike, get to the hitting area and take your chance.

**11.** Find the pitched ball early, while it is still in the pitcher's hand. Do not wait to find the ball as it is in flight to the plate. Find the pitcher's release point prior to getting to the plate and focus on that area as the pitcher delivers the ball. Hitting the ball is hard enough; letting the ball travel without getting sight of the pitch will make it that much harder.

**12.** Do not let the arms get fully extended until the bat and swing reach is too long. Extending the arms early will also limit the adjustments a hitter can make during the swing.

**13.** Make sure the body weight stays back throughout the swing. A hitter who allows the body weight to shift forward will struggle with off-speed pitches. Keeping control of the body weight is hard, but necessary to make a proper swing.

**14.** Just as the feet need to move slowly, the hands need to be quick—not jerky, but quick, smooth and direct to the ball. As the bat moves into the contact area, accelerating bat speed should be generated. Quick hands will aid in this process.

**15.** Get good extension at the end of the swing. Do not let the arms and swing stop at contact. Let the bat finish naturally with an extension of the arms though the ball. A swing that is cut off will result in loss of power.

**16.** As the weight of the body is shifted to a firm front leg, make sure the back foot pivot allows for the rotation of the upper body. Remember to "smoosh the bug." A back foot leaving the ground during contact will cause the hitter to lose most of the power produced by the swing.

**17.** Try to decide early if the ball is a strike or ball. Do your very best to swing only at strikes. Do not let your aggressiveness get the best of you. Stay back, decide if the ball is a strike and let the bat fly. Swinging at bad pitches and making the strike zone bigger than it is will set a hitter up for failure. Know the strike zone and swing only at the hittable pitches.

**18.** Keep the head steady. Tracking the ball is very hard, so do not let the head shift during the swing. Build the mechanics of the swing to allow the head to find the ball and keep sight of the pitch early and uninterrupted throughout the swing. A swing that allows the head to move is a recipe for failure.

# 4

# Strategies

# Hitting in the Count

Every pitch puts the hitter in a different position. The first pitch in the count is the pitcher's chance to get ahead; at the same time, the hitter will be looking to get a good strike to hit. If the pitch is a ball, the pitcher will now need to throw a strike to get back to even in the count. The hitter is now looking at a fastball count and a hittable pitch. We know the hitter walks on four balls, and strikes out on the three strikes. The pitcher has a plan to get the hitter out, and the hitter should have a plan on how to get a hit. With runners on base, the pitcher will make adjustments, just as the hitter does. Each pitch and each situation plays an important role in the plan of the hitter and of the pitcher.

Be aggressive; do not wait for something to happen. Be positive and concentrate on getting a hit. Do not go to the plate with the thought that the pitcher is too tough for you. A hitter who goes to the plate hoping just to survive will not have any success. Take charge and be confident that a base hit or hard hit ball is going to result from that at-bat. A good mental approach is the key to a successful hitter.

Let's take a look at the different counts and the basic concepts behind each pitch. These are just general rules, as a hitter should always be ready for a fastball, and be able to adjust to the off-speed pitch.

## 0-0 COUNT:

In this count a pitcher is trying to get ahead in the count. Normally a pitcher will throw the fastball. The location of this pitch is generally over a big portion of the plate. The pitcher always wants to stay ahead. Occasionally, an off-speed pitcher may throw hit most consistent pitch. If the pitcher is a changeup pitcher, a changeup getting a big portion of the plate is very common. As a hitter, do not overswing. Look for a pitch that is hard and over the plate. Do not get anxious and swing at a pitch out of the strike zone. There are many pitches left in this at-bat.

### 0-1 COUNT:

This count finds the hitter behind in the count. There are many pitches left in the at-bat, so again do not get anxious. The pitcher is still trying to throw a strike, but the pitcher has now sectioned the plate into three: inside, outside, and middle. The outside or inside corner will be the target area. If the pitcher has an off-speed pitch they can throw for a strike, this would be the time to throw it, but the fastball to the inside or outside corner is still the pitch of choice. The pitcher will still attempt to keep this pitch down in the strike zone. Normally a fastball to the outside corner is most common in this count. A hitter needs to try to get a good pitch and to drive the ball hard to the field based on the position of the pitch in the strike zone. Still look for a ball you can drive with authority.

### 0-2 COUNT:

This count is the in the pitcher's favor. They are way ahead and have plenty of pitches to waste if needed. This count is when the pitcher will try to throw a pitch just off the plate to see if the hitter will chase it, or a pitch up and out of the strike zone to get a swing. The pitcher will sometimes try to throw the off-speed pitch again, out of the strike zone, to get a swing. As a hitter, a little shorter swing with a focus on contact is needed. The homerun swing is not the swing in this situation. A quick, smooth swing with balance and a line-drive approach is what you should look for.

## 1-2 COUNT:

This count is still a pitcher's count. The hitter can usually look for the off-speed pitch or the second-best pitch a pitcher has. The fastball will still be off the plate looking for the hitter to chase the pitch. The inside pitch is very common here. The pitcher will look to move the hitter off the plate with a pitch in off the plate. This inside pitch will set up the 2-2 pitch.

The 1-2 count is the last count the pitcher can actively try to strike out the hitter. After this count the pitcher needs to try to get the hitter to put the ball in play. As a hitter, the swing should still be short with an eye on contact. The swing should be more of a contact-type swing. If the pitcher makes a mistake and throws the ball in the middle of the plate, driving this ball into the gap is perfect.

## 2-2 COUNT:

This count gives the advantage to the hitter. The pitcher will try to put this pitch in play and throw this ball over the plate. The pitcher does not want to work the count to 3-2 where a walk can happen. The 2-2 pitch will be the pitcher's most consistent strike pitch. If the pitcher feels the fastball is the best pitch that day the fastball will be thrown. If throwing a different pitch for strikes is the best, then the pitcher will be throwing that pitch.

The location of this pitch is much like the 0-0 pitch. The pitcher will get the ball over a large part of the plate. As a hitter, trying to drive this ball is fine. If the ball is in the middle of the plate and slightly up in the strike zone, driving this ball is perfect. If the pitcher is able to keep the ball out of the middle of the plate, a line drive short swing is the proper approach. The overswing will cause a pop-up or weak ground ball. Be careful not to chase the pitch out of the strike zone. Remember, the pitcher needs to throw a strike.

## 1-0 COUNT:

This is a hitter's count. The pitcher is behind in the count and needs to throw a strike. A fastball getting a big part of the plate is the normal pitch. A pitcher does not want to get fancy here and fall to 2-0. Very seldom will a pitcher throw an off-speed pitch or look to throw the pitch on the corner. As a hitter, look to hit the ball hard. Pick a portion of the plate that you feel you can hit the ball well and look for that area. If the ball is in the expected area try to make the pitcher pay. Be real careful not to get too aggressive and chase ball 2.

## 2-0 COUNT:

This is the best count for a hitter to get a good hit. Unlike all the other counts, the hitter is definitely in the driver's seat. Find a location in the strike zone that can be handled by your swing and sit on that area. The fastball is most likely coming so be prepared for it. The pitcher does not want to get to 3-0 under any circumstance so a strike down the middle is most likely. If this pitch is not a fastball, lay off the pitch. No need to chase any pitch that is not perfect to hit, for there are many pitches left in this at bat. Be sure to stay relaxed and try not to overswing.

## 1-1 COUNT:

Nobody has the advantage here. This is the pitch where the pitcher is trying to get back ahead but is not really in the situation where the middle of the plate is the target. The inside and outside corner is the pitcher's target. It is not uncommon for the pitcher to throw a curve or slider, maybe even a change, if the pitcher is able to locate the pitch. The hitter can look to drive the ball if a mistake is thrown or if the pitcher throws to the area the hitter is looking for. Be careful not to chase the ball up in the strike zone. There are plenty of pitches left in the at bat; don't chase a pitcher's pitch.

## 2-1 COUNT:

This is a hitter's count. The pitcher does not want to run the count to 3-1 so a strike is coming. A fastball here is most likely, normally to get a big part of the plate. In this count a hitter needs to try to be productive. The hitter has worked the pitcher to a position where a good pitch to hit is common. Look for the fastball here and get a good balanced solid swing. Don't let the pitcher trick you with a bad pitch. Be patient and try to drive the ball into the outfield. In this situation, looking for the pitch in a certain area is fine.

## 3-1 COUNT:

This is one of the few times where the pressure is all on the pitcher. One bad pitch and a walk is drawn. A pitcher is almost forced to throw the fastball down the middle. If for some reason a pitcher can throw an off-speed pitch in the strike zone, let it go. Don't get yourself out on a pitcher's pitch. Give the pitcher credit for coming up with the perfect pitch. As a hitter, be sure to get a good swing if the ball is down the middle. Do not let yourself be overaggressive. Make sure the ball is just where you can handle it and get a good swing.

### 3-0 COUNT:

This is the hitter's count for sure. A pitcher has to throw a strike or walk the hitter. Normally, unless one is a homerun hitter with the OK of the coach, the hitter is not swinging in this count. The hitter is taking this pitch, even if it is right down the middle. If the coach gives the OK to swing, make sure the pitch is a fastball right down the middle. There is no need to help the pitcher and get out with the count this far in the hitter's favor.

Summing up, keep these simple rules in mind. When hitting ahead in the count, look for a fastball. Find a section of the zone to hit in and make a good swing when the pitch is in that section. Be selective when ahead in the count, because the pitcher has to throw a strike. When behind in the count, shorten up the swing. Be protective at the plate. The pitcher that is ahead in the count does not need to throw a fastball or a strike. Concentrate on putting the ball in play with a good swing.

## Situational Hitting

We just talked about the different counts and the way a pitcher is trying to work the strike zone. We will now add to the count by adding runners and outs. Remember that every hitter is not the same. It would be nice to hit just based on where the ball is in the strike zone, but to be effective, hitters need to hit to their individual strengths. A power hitter should not try to bunt on a regular basis, and a line drive hitter should not be trying to hit home runs. The following information is for a hitter to be aware of and try to incorporate into the game. It is not mandatory, especially for the young hitter just trying to make solid contact. With no runners on base, the hitter should try to make contact based on the type of hitter they are. The hitter should realize that it is very hard to score from home plate, so make a good swing and get on base for the hitters coming up behind them. Let the hitters hitting behind you do their job and drive you in. Get a good pitch and put a good swing on it. Use the information given on hitting in the count and be aggressive.

## RUNNER ON FIRST

With a man on first, the hitter's job is to move the runner into scoring position—second or third base. Get a good pitch and try to hit it hard. If possible, the hitter should look for a pitch that can be hit to the outfield on the ground so the runner can reach second base. If the hitter can get a pitch that can be hit to the right field side, the runner will have a chance to reach third if the ball reaches the outfield. There are far more ways to score from third than from second. Do not swing at a bad pitch. Swinging at a bad pitch will result in a ground ball and a possible double play. Runner on first and no outs is a common bunt situation. In this case, the hitter's job is to give up the at-bat and sacrifice the runner to second base by bunting. The coach always signals the bunt play. A hitter will never sacrifice without a signal, because the runner on base needs to know a bunt play is on. Do not try to drag bunt, put the ball in play and allow the runner to move up to second base.

Runner on first with one out is normally not a bunt play. If this situation comes up late in a close game, a bunt may be needed to move the runner, but early in the game no bunt is needed. In this situation the hitter is looking to hit the ball hard on the ground or line drive to get on base. A fly ball will do nothing to help the runner advance. If the runner on base has speed, the hitter may let a pitch or two go by, allowing the runner to steal second base. If the runner can steal second during your at-bat, you may be able to get a hit and score the runner. Do not take so many pitches that you can put yourself in a hole at 0-2 or worse. Giving the runner a pitch to run, and putting yourself down in the count 0-1, is not a bad situation.

## RUNNER ON THIRD

Coming to bat with a man on third is a great situation. If you can hit the ball into the outfield, the runner should score easily. With a man on third, the hitter needs to hit the ball to the first-base side of the field to allow the runner to score while the defense throws to first for the out. Although you are thrown out, a run will score, and that is a great trade. Taking a big swing and hitting the ball in the air is not productive at all. Stay under control and drive the ball on the ground. If you do get a pitch that is very hittable, driving the ball to the outfield is great. A fly ball to the deep portion of the outfield will usually be more than enough for the runner to tag up and score. Almost anytime that you can trade an out for a run, is good for the team.

Occasionally, with a runner on third and less than two outs, a bunt is the proper play. The coach will also tell the runner to run as soon as the pitcher releases the ball. This combination of actions is called a squeeze play. This is a risky play; if the pitch is not bunted the catcher almost always tags the runner out. If the hitter can get the ball on the ground, a run is scored. This bunt is not a drag bunt for a base hit. This is a sacrifice bunt with no attempt at reaching first base unless the defense makes an error.

With the runner on third and two outs, a sacrifice or a ground ball to the defense is of no help to the team. With only one out remaining in the inning, the hitter needs to reach base. Get a good pitch to hit and drive the ball somewhere. Keep in mind that a bad pitch the catcher cannot handle will result in the runner scoring from third without contact from the hitter. Be patient and do not chase the ball out of the strike zone.

## RUNNER ON SECOND

With a man on second and less than two outs, the hitter can hit the ball on the ground to the first base side and the runner can move to third. The perfect situation would be for the hitter to hit the ball to right field so the runner can score from second base. The base hit to left field is fine, but the runner will find it hard to score because the runner has to wait for the ball to get past the infield defense before running. The hit to right field is the ball that the runner can score on because they can start running at contact. Usually, the hit to center field is good because again the runner can take off running from contact. The fly ball to left or center will not allow the runner to advance to third, but the fly ball to right field will move the runner up. The fly to right field will be too far a throw for the outfielder to have a good chance to throw the runner out advancing to third. Very seldom will the hitter be asked to move the runner to third with a bunt. In a close game with no outs a bunt may be called to get the runner to third, where they can score on a sacrifice fly later.

## BASES LOADED

The best and most productive situation for the hitter is bases loaded and less than two outs. In this situation, the pitcher cannot afford to walk the hitter. This means the hitter will see strikes. Find a pitch that can be driven. A fly ball to the outfield will score the runner from third. A base hit will most likely score two runners. The double will score three runs. If the pitcher gets behind in the count, look for a pitch that is in the middle portion of the plate. The pitcher behind in the count needs to make sure they throw strikes. If the count is 2-0 or 3-1, a homerun-type pitch is a possibility. This is not a bunt situation. There are too many good things that can happen with a hit to give up a hitter by bunting.

Early in the game, the coach is usually not as concerned with strategic moves. The hitter should be more interested in hitting the ball and reaching base. As the game moves on and the score adds up, the outs become more important and the runners have to be given extra attention. The hitter who gets a chance to come up with runners late in the game needs to keep the situation in mind.

Do what you can to help the team win the game. Be sure always to get a good pitch, and make a good swing. Different hitters are capable of doing different things. Play *your* game, based on the skills *you* have. Trying to do too much will result in failure. Remember the pitcher has to throw strikes; do not help the pitcher by swinging at pitches out of the strike zone.

# 5

# Other Skills for the Hitter

## Bunting

Bunting is an important part of hitting. There are two types of bunting: the sacrifice bunt and the drag bunt.

The sacrifice bunt is designed to advance the runner to the next base, and is signaled by the coach to the hitter. A hitter will almost never sacrifice bunt without the call from the coach. The first move when attempting a sacrifice bunt is to position your body properly. Do this by pivoting your back foot toward the pitcher. Turn your back foot so that the toes are facing the mound. Now, slide your top hand up the bat, approximately to the label. The bottom hand should then slide to the top of the handle. Also, a correct grip of the bat will find you wrapping your thumb around the bat with your top hand, while the bottom hand holds the bat just as you would in a normal swing.

*Proper bunt position*

The next move is to raise the head of the bat above the hands. This is done to help control the bat. The barrel should always be at the top of the strike zone when attempting to bunt the ball. The objective is to catch the ball with the bat. Be sure to keep your head facing the ball and the

*Incorrect bunt position*

bat in front of the plate. If you fail to extend the bat in front of the plate, the ball will be bunted foul. The upper body should be turned so that the chest is facing the pitcher. Be sure to square the body to the pitcher early to get the body in position to bunt the ball fair. If the body is not turned to the pitcher, the bat will not be out in front of the strike zone and the ball will beat the bat to the plate. Try to bunt the ball between the mound and the first base line. This is the best location for the sacrifice bunt. The best bunts roll close to the base line, but stay fair.

A sacrifice is considered successful if someone other than the pitcher fields the ball. Even if the pitcher does field the ball, the sacrifice can still be successful if the ball was not bunted directly to the pitcher, and they had to hustle to get the ball and make the play. The proper sacrifice bunt will land and stay in a triangular area at each side of the pitching mound. If the bunt stays in these areas, the runner is sure to advance to the next base.

If a hitter attempts a sacrifice bunt with a runner on third and less than two outs, the bunt is called a squeeze play. This is a very risky play because if the ball is missed, the runner (who will run when the pitch is released) is

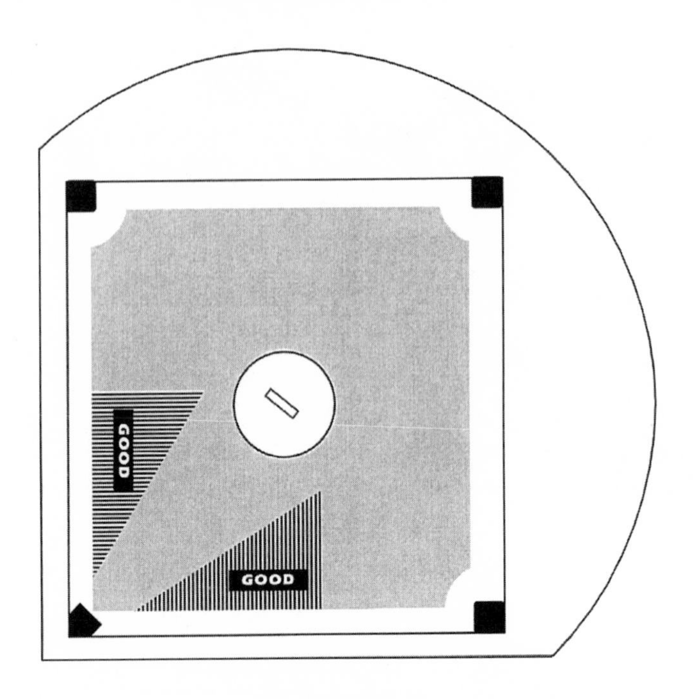


*Sacrifice bunt areas*

almost an out for sure. The hitter needs to do everything possible to bunt the ball, regardless of whether the pitch is a strike or ball. If the ball is bunted fair the runner from third will score most of the time. Be sure not to turn around too early and signal the bunt to the pitcher. If the pitcher notices the squeeze play, they will throw a pitch that is impossible to bunt and the catcher will tag the runner attempting to score. Let the pitcher's front leg land on the ground before any move is made. This will ensure that the pitcher cannot make an adjustment on the pitch.

The other type of bunt is the "drag bunt," which is used to attempt a base hit. This type of bunt is used by the hitter with excellent running speed, or as a surprise to the defense that is not ready to defend the bunt. We will first discuss the drag bunt technique for the right-handed hitter. The first move is to drop the back foot instead of pivoting on it. This is done by stepping about one foot backward and six inches away from the plate. Next, slide your top hand up the bat while starting to move out of the batter's box toward first base. Do not let the top hand get more than halfway up the bat at contact. A hand that gets too far up the bat will risk getting hit at contact with the pitched ball. Remember, it is illegal to make contact with a pitched ball while out of the batter's box. Be sure to stay in the box until contact is made. Make sure the head of the bat is in front of the plate in the strike zone. Unlike the sacrifice bunt, the grip on the top hand is not with just the thumb, but with the fingers wrapped fully around the bat. Be sure to grip the bat at the label. This manner of grip is used to help disguise the drag bunt from the defense. Watch the ball make contact with the bat as you begin to run down the base line.

*Position for a drag bunt*

The left-handed hitter attempting the drag bunt should first bring the back foot around toward the plate as the ball is in flight. As the ball approaches the strike zone, slide the hand up the bat. This will allow the hitter to drop the head of the bat in front of the plate in the contact area. Make contact with the pitch as you start to run up the baseline. Be sure to make contact while your body is still in the batter's box. Do not spend time looking to see if the ball is fair or foul; just run full speed.

Do not give the drag bunt away to the defense by rotating the body too early; let the pitcher release the ball before any move in the batter's box. A good drag bunter can wait for the ball to be halfway to the plate before making a move. Normally the hitter, not the coach, decides a drag bunt. A hitter needs to decide if they can make the bunt for a base hit. It is helpful to check the position of the infielders before attempting the drag bunt. Make sure the corner infielders are in a position deep enough for you to beat the throw to first base. Pay attention to where the pitcher finishes the pitch. Check to see if the pitcher falls off to the first or third base side of the mound. This will help in deciding which direction to bunt the ball. Otherwise, the bunt will result in an easy out.

## Base Running

Base running is an important skill for a hitter. After contact is made, the hitter becomes a base runner. Be sure to get a good swing with proper mechanics, and then worry about running the bases later.

There are many different situations that can arise while circling the bases. We will cover the most common situations that will happen in the course of the game. No matter what the situation, be sure to watch the base coach. His job is to direct the runners around the bases. Something that cannot be base-coached is hustle—be sure to be an aggressive base runner, regardless of the situation.

## INFIELD HIT

The proper strategy when running out the infield grounder is to run "through" the base. Run as fast as you can down the base line, not slowing until you have run 10 to 15 feet past the first base bag. This is referred to as "through" the bag. Do not slow down unless directed to do so by the base coach. Be sure to tag the base near the center; this will avoid twisting your ankle. Do not step on the inside portion of the base. This area is for the first baseman. Attempting to touch the base in this area will result in a collision and someone will end up hurt. There is a restraining area that needs to be used as your path to first base. If the ball hits the runner while the runner is outside the restraining area, the runner will be called out for interference.

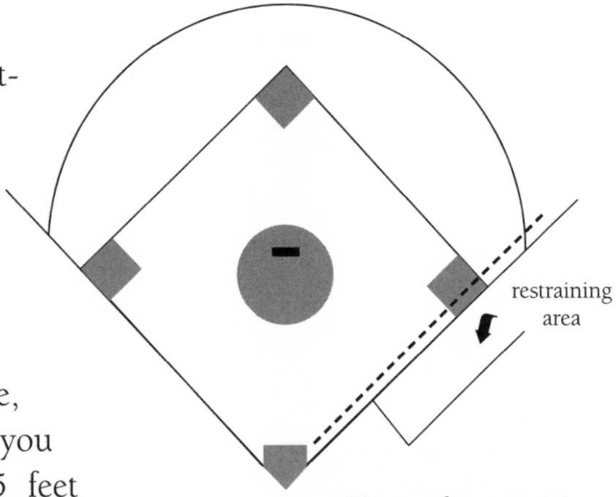

restraining area

*Keep to the restraining area on an infield hit*

## BASE HIT

Make sure the ball has been hit through the infield and the base coach is signaling to round the base. Round the bag on a base hit, which will help you see the field and judge whether to take the extra base on a misplayed ball. To

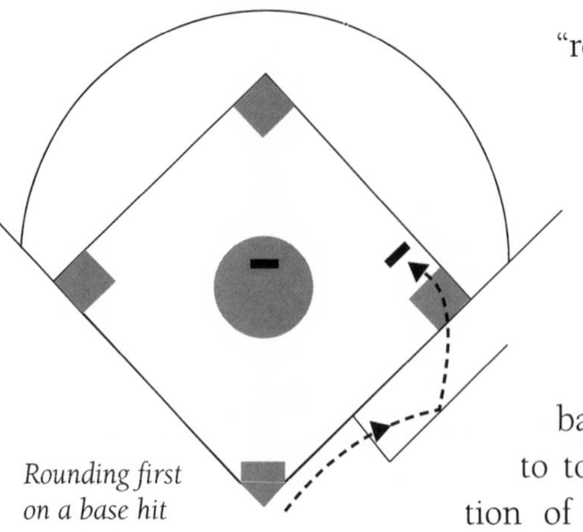

*Rounding first on a base hit*

"round the bag" means to run hard to the start of the restraining line. At this point, break toward the coach's box and then back to the base to allow yourself to touch the inside portion of the first base bag. This will put the runner in the best position to head for the next base, if necessary. After touching the base it is best to continue four or five steps toward the next base, just in case the ball is misplayed and you can advance to the next base. If the ball is played correctly and the ball is thrown to the next base, you can easily return to the base just reached. Be sure not to run so hard that you are out of control. It is important to run hard, but just as important is control of your body as you round the bases.

## EXTRA BASES

This style of base running is much like running out the base hit, except you will continue to run past first base and head for second. If you hit a double and there is no chance to advance to third, there is no need to run past second base. If the ball is hit and it is not known if a triple is possible, as you reach second continue past the base by rounding just as was done at first base. This same technique is used again at third when a triple is hit or if a runner has a chance to score. Be sure to check with the base coaches as you circle the bases. They have a much better look at the field than you do and they can direct you.

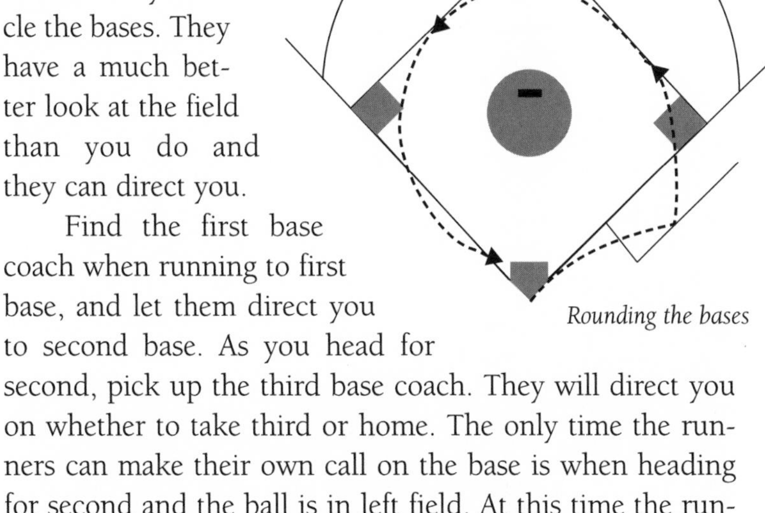
Rounding the bases

Find the first base coach when running to first base, and let them direct you to second base. As you head for second, pick up the third base coach. They will direct you on whether to take third or home. The only time the runners can make their own call on the base is when heading for second and the ball is in left field. At this time the runner can see the play and can decide when to stop.

## Sliding

Sliding is one of the most important base running techniques.* As you head toward the base on a hit, the first move in attempting a slide is to jump off the right foot into the air. Do not slow down to perform a slide. Maintain your running speed. While in the air, bend your right knee under your body and extend the left leg. As your body approaches the ground, raise your hands upward so they are not

*In professional baseball, sliding can also include a head-first slide. *A head-first slide is not recommended, however, as it is very dangerous.* Your hand, wrist, or fingers can easily be injured. Therefore, this slide will not be covered.

caught under the body. As the left foot touches the base, lean forward. This will cause the body to pop upright as you hit the base. This will put the runner in position to run to the next base if a bad throw is made. This slide is referred to as the "pop-up" slide. The slide should begin well before the base, though an exact distance cannot be specified. The distance depends upon the speed of the runner and the hardness of the ground. The faster the runner, the longer the distance needed to perform the slide.

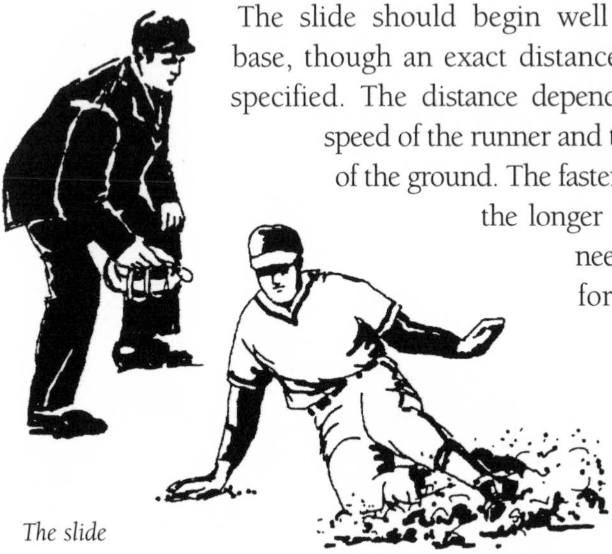

*The slide*

Base running is much like every other aspect of baseball. You will have to practice to improve. Running speed is a real advantage, especially when trying to steal a base. Very seldom does a runner steal a base without the slide.

# 6

# Common Problems

# Bucket Stride

As we discussed earlier, the proper stride makes sure the stride foot is on the ground at contact and that the stride is toward the pitcher's belt buckle. The proper stride allows the front side of the hitter, especially the front shoulder, to stay closed. In the bucket stride, the hitter does not stride to the pitcher's belt. Instead, the stride is to the base line. This causes the front shoulder to open too early and the ability to cover the strike zone is limited. This stride is usually caused because the hitter is worried about getting hit by the pitch, or the hitter is trying too hard to hit the ball to the pull field. When this stride happens the hitter needs to concentrate on the front foot striding in the proper position. It is sometimes helpful to take some swings with no stride to work through the problem.

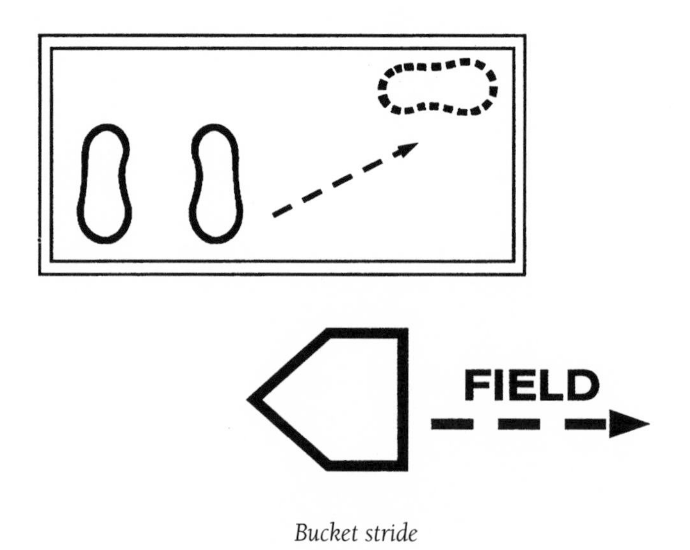


*Bucket stride*

## Broom Swing

This is sometimes referred to as the sweeping swing. This swing will not allow the hitter to catch up to a good fastball and also limit ability the hitter has to make adjustments. This swing happens when the hitter's front arm becomes fully extended very early in the swing. The stiff arm will extend the bat too far in the strike zone, leaving a good portion of the inside part of the plate open for the pitcher to throw for a strike without the hitter being able to make contact. The over-extended swing is normally corrected when the hitter works on the backstop drill (p. 123) where the shadow swings are performed against a backstop or fence. The hitter needs to be sure that there is always some bend in the elbows through the swing, not letting the extension of the arms occur until the hitter is finishing the swing beyond the contact area.

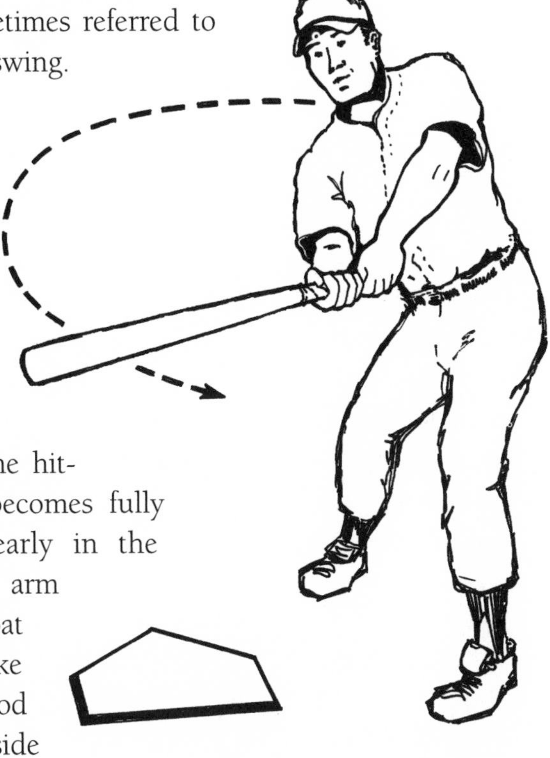

*Over-extended front elbow in a broom swing*

## Loop Swing

We discussed earlier that the proper swing occurs when the swing track is slightly downward, making contact with the ball on the top half of the ball. Hitting the center portion of the ball is also acceptable, but hitting the bottom half of the ball is never recommended. The loop swing happens when the hitter drops the hands early in the swing, and the swing track becomes an uppercut swing. With the uppercut swing, the hitter cannot hit the ball on the upper half of the ball. The only contact area is the bottom half. The hitter needs to work hard on keeping the hands high through the swing track, making sure the downward plane is achieved. The uppercut swing will find the hitter struggling to make contact, resulting in lots of swings and misses.

*Track of a loop swing*

## Hand Hitch

The hand hitch is the act of the hitter dropping the hands as a first move when starting the swing into the swing track. The hand hitch usually develops because the hitter is not strong enough to swing the bat. Hitters very often try to use a bat too heavy for them, and this causes them to try to muscle the swing. The hand hitch may also happen at the trigger when the hitter jerks the hands back or forward prior to the start of the swing. Remember, the proper hand action is a smooth, easy start with directness to the track. To cure a hand hitch the hitter needs to do plenty of shadow swings, working very hard on the hand action during the trigger.

*Sequence of a hand hitch, left to right*

# Pulling Off

The hitter in a proper swing keeps the front shoulder pointed at the pitcher throughout the swing, from start to finish. The hitter who lifts the head out of the swing and lets the chin get over the shoulder will often pull off the ball. The chin needs to stay inside the shoulder so the hitter can keep their eyes on the ball during the swing. The hitter who allows the chin outside the shoulder will start to fall off the swing, which is referred to as pulling off the ball. When the head gets outside the front shoulder, the body will follow and the swing will fall apart. Very often the hitter pulling off the ball will swing and miss often and have no chance to hit the ball from the middle of the strike zone to the outside portion of the plate. The hitter with this problem needs to spend time trying to hit the ball to the opposite field. In order to hit the ball to the opposite field, the hitter has to keep the head and chin on the pitch.

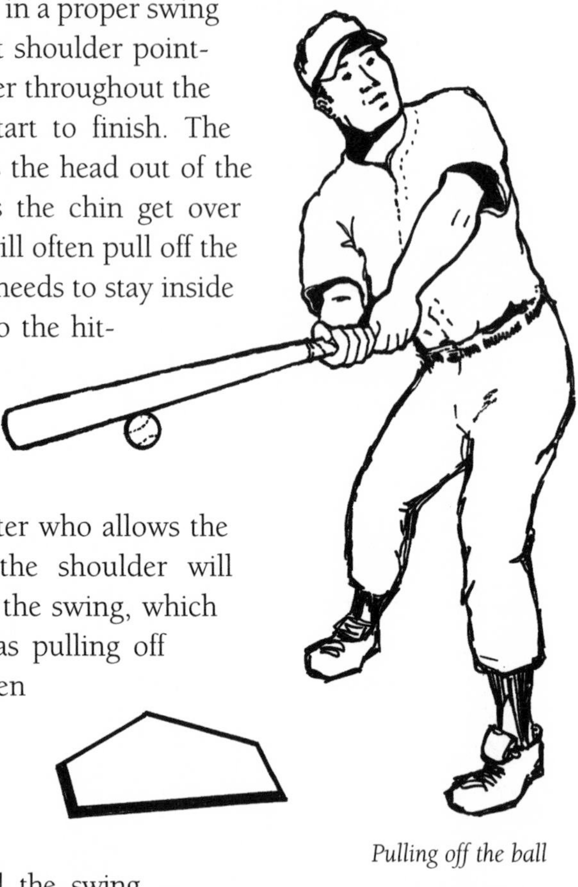

*Pulling off the ball*

## Knee Break

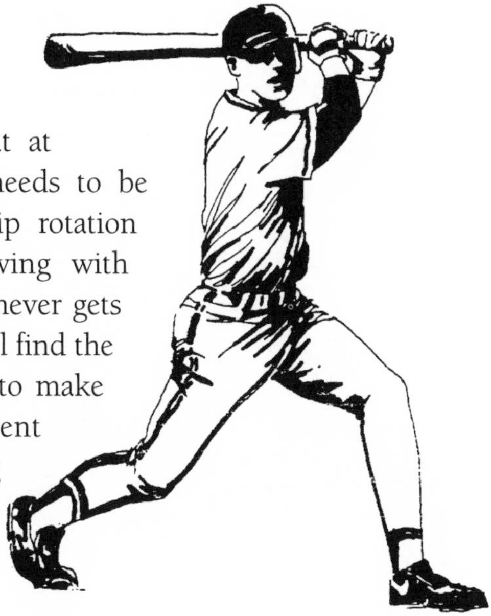

The hitter making the correct swing has a little flex in the knees early in the swing, but at contact the front leg needs to be firm to support the hip rotation needed to make a swing with power. The hitter who never gets to the firm front side will find the head moves too much to make consistent contact. Bent knees during the swing will cause the head to move up and down, making it very hard for the hitter to track the pitched ball correctly. There needs to be some flex in the back knee, but the hitter who has a severely bent back knee will cause the swing to uppercut. This as discussed earlier is a cause for problems. Start the swing with the flex in the knees but firm up the front side as contact occurs.

*Front knee break*

## No Backside Rotation

The back foot needs to make a rotation to face the pitcher. The hitter who does not rotate the back foot will limit the amount of power a hitter can generate to the upper body. The lower body is essential to create power. The lower body is locked in place if the back foot cannot rotate. As a

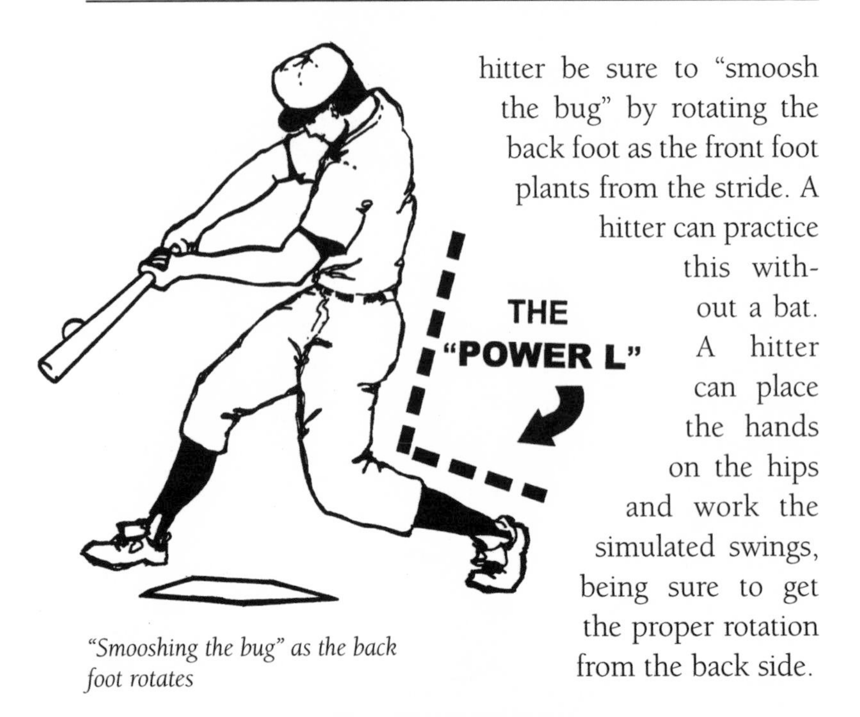


"Smooshing the bug" as the back foot rotates

hitter be sure to "smoosh the bug" by rotating the back foot as the front foot plants from the stride. A hitter can practice this without a bat. A hitter can place the hands on the hips and work the simulated swings, being sure to get the proper rotation from the back side.

## Overstriding

A hitter needs to keep the bottom half of the body under control. Very often the hitter will get too spread out during the swing; this is caused by a hitter striding too far. A hitter needs to be sure that the stride is under control and direct to the belt buckle of the pitcher. Understriding is a better mistake than overstriding. The hitter who overstrides will again get to the contact area from the bottom half of the ball. Because the hitter is overstriding the hitter will be slow making adjustments. To repair this problem, draw a line in the batter's box where the stride should be, prior to getting set up. Do not look at the stride line during the swing, but the fact that the line is there will often cause the hitter to be aware of the problem and help correct the trouble.

## Too Aggressive

This is a common problem for hitters at all levels. Hitters from time to time get so anxious that they cannot stay back and wait for the pitch. Usually this problem happens when a hitter is struggling or not seeing the ball well. Overly aggressive hitting never happens when a hitter is hitting well or feels comfortable in the box. Be sure as a hitter to let nothing happen until the pitcher releases the ball. Make sure to see the ball and relax as the swing develops. Too often the hitter who is struggling will try to do too much too early and wind up failing. Take a deep breath and let the body perform the swing. Do not try to force the swing. Let the swing develop smoothly and naturally. There is plenty of time, give yourself a chance to drive the ball.

# 7

# Practice Drills

## Shadow Swings

Every player ever to swing a bat has performed this drill. It can be a great learning tool if done correctly, but more often than not, players usually just go through the motions. To do this drill, set your feet as if you were in the batter's box awaiting the pitched ball. Imagine the pitch approaching the plate. Practice your footwork and swing, paying special attention to the proper swing track and hand placement. Imagine different pitches being thrown. Practice the proper swing if a curveball or slider were the pitch. Work on the type of swing needed when behind in the count or work on the drag bunt footwork. This drill is also very helpful if performed in front of the mirror so you can see the problems that occur during the swing.

## Short Toss

This drill requires one additional player to aid in tossing the pitch. This is an outstanding drill that can aid in developing hand-eye coordination and bat speed. This drill will also help a hitter clear up footwork problems. Hopefully a backstop is available, but if not a net will speed up the drill. This drill starts with the hitter getting into the stance as if a pitch were being thrown. Get the bat in the proper position ·ready to make a swing. The other player needs to kneel on one knee beside you, out of the reach of the bat during the swing, at the front line of the opposite batter's box, in a position slightly out in front of the hitter. From here, lightly toss the ball underhand, knee-high in the strike zone, allowing the hitter to make solid contact in the contact area. The hitter will make the proper swing and

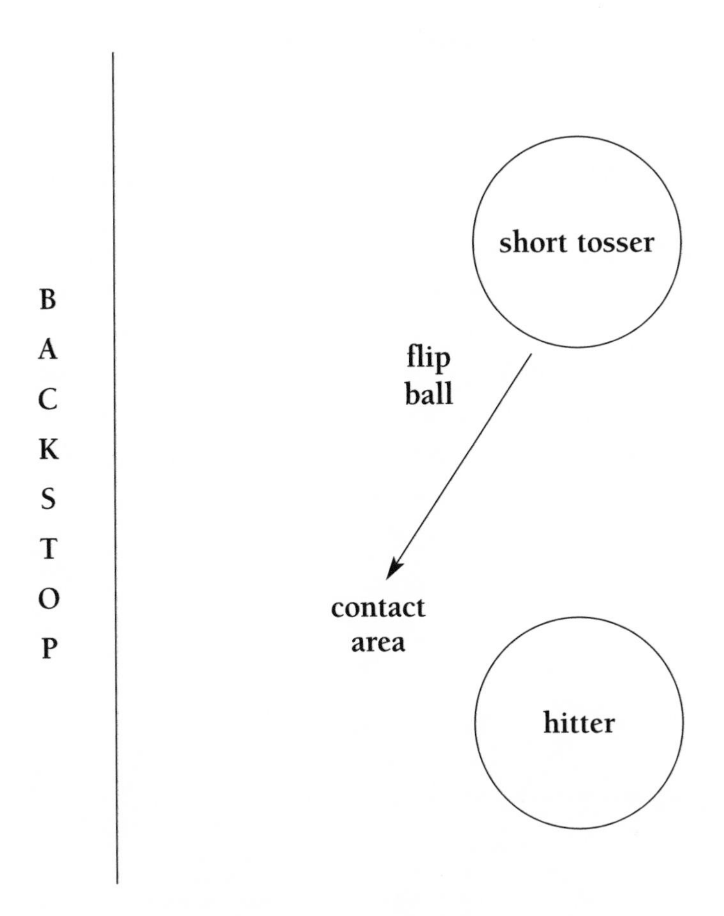


*Short toss drill*

drive the ball into the backstop or net. If performed on the field the ball should be a line drive or hard ground ball up the middle. The soft toss person should try to throw the ball in different sections of the contact area so the hitter can practice the different types of swings needed to be effective.

## Batting Tee Drill

Almost every player has performed this drill. In fact, younger players typically use this batting aid to produce offense instead of using a pitcher. It's important to remember that although the base of the tee looks like a home plate, it is only a base and should not be used as the actual home plate when setting up the stance. The proper position of the tee is one foot forward of the actual home plate on the field. This is where the actual contact should be made.

On all these drills, make sure to concentrate on your footwork and balance. Set your feet in the batter's box as if a pitch were coming. Set the hands and prepare for the swing.

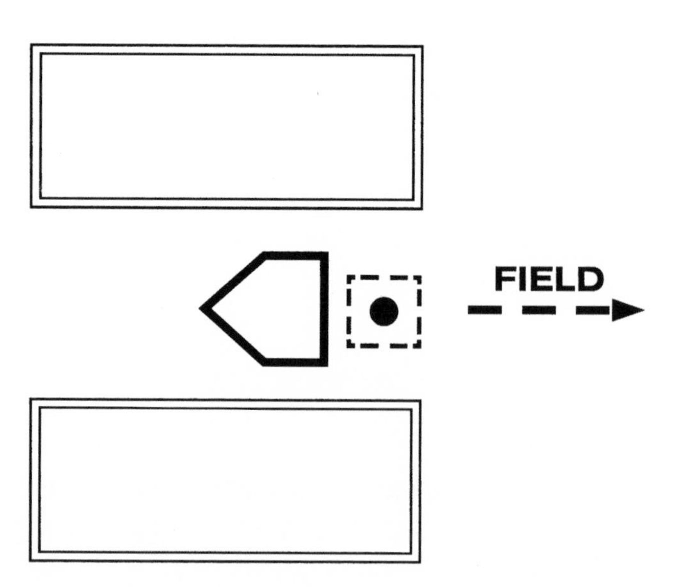


*Proper tee position for the tee drill*

With the batting tee properly set in the contact area, make a swing, working on the proper mechanics of the swing. Move the tee around the contact area to work on different pitches in different areas. The batting tee is very good for the hitter who needs work on the pitch on the outside half of the plate.

## Backstop Swing

Working with the same idea as the shadow swings, the hitter needs to set up to the backstop or fence. The back of the dugout can also be used for this drill. Set the feet paral-

*Backstop or wall drill*

lel to the fence or wall; the distance from the fence or wall is decided by the length of the bat. Put the knob of the bat against the bellybutton and extend the bat to the fence. When the end of the bat is touching or nearly touching the fence this is the proper distance. Now, set the bat in the loaded position with feet ready to hit. Practice the shadow swings, making sure not to strike the wall or fence during the swing. This drill is very god for the hitter with trouble keeping the hands inside the ball. This drill is also good for the hitter that has a sweeping swing and needs to work to shorten the swing. The backstop drill is not designed to be a rapid swing drill. Take your time and work on developing a better swing.

## Fungo Drill

This drill is good for the hitter who has problems hitting the upper portion of the ball in a downward plane. The hitter needs to get the fungo bat from the coach. A fungo bat is used by the coach for hitting infield ground balls and outfield flies during practice. It's a long, thin bat with a narrow barrel. Take this bat and set up in the hitting position. Get the bat in the proper position, ready to make the swing. With the bottom hand, lightly toss a ball in the air to the contact area and swing the fungo to make contact for a ground ball. Because the bat is so narrow, the hitter will need to concentrate hard just to make contact. The hitter will find that after hitting ground balls with the fungo, hitting with the actual bat is much easier. The fungo will aid in learning a downward type swing, and sharpen the batting eye of the hitter.

## Whiffle Ball Drill

Taking batting practice with whiffle balls instead of real baseballs is helpful when space is limited. This drill will also work the hitter's ability to stay back and have patience. Unlike the real baseballs, the whiffle ball will come at a much slower speed, so the hitter needs to work on staying back and not rushing the swing. The pitcher will be at a much shorter distance than the actual pitching mound. The hitter will see the ball just as usual, but at contact the ball will not travel as far, making it easier to retrieve the balls. It is also helpful to develop the hitting eye if golf ball-sized plastic balls are used. This will aid in the concentration at contact.

## Weighted Bat

Working on the swing with a bat that is heavier than the actual game bat is helpful when working on practice swings. When working shadow swings with the weighted bat, the hitter will naturally shorten the swing track and thus aid in quickening the swing. Because the weighted bat is heavy, the hitter will work the swing with a short track. This will help the hitter when trying to make contact with the lighter game bat. They heavy bat should be only four to five ounces heavier than the game bat. This weighted bat is not recommended for batting practice, because hitting live pitches with the heavy bat will cause the hitter to lengthen the swing and cause a slow bat.

## Double Tee Drill

Much like the tee drill discussed earlier, set up at the plate with the batting tee slightly ahead of the plate in the

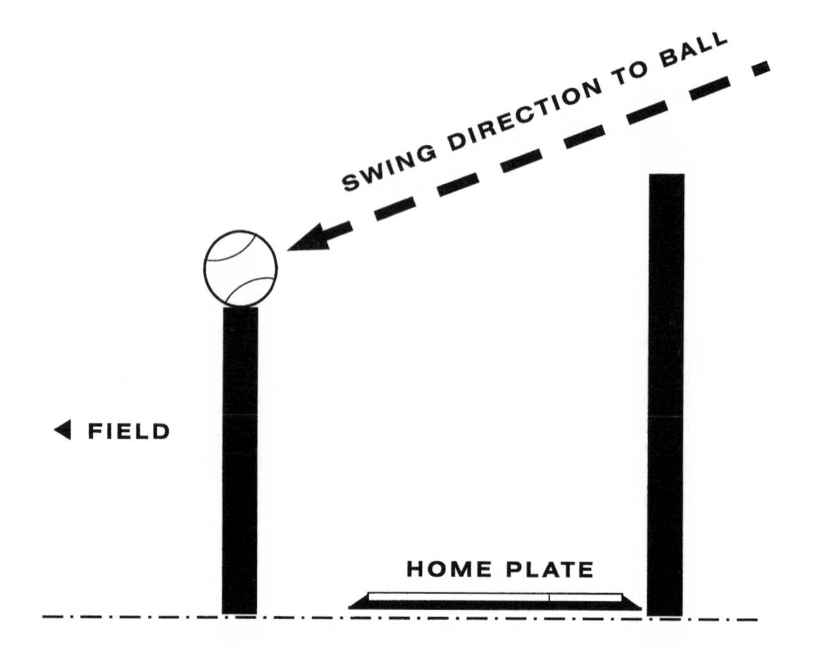


*Setup for the double tee drill*

contact area. Set another tee at the back half of the plate with the tee set up about 5 inches higher than the front tee. Put a ball on the front tee to be hit by the swing. The back tee being set higher than the front will encourage a downward swing working the bat track into the strike zone. The back tee should not be too high or the swing will become a chop swing. Make some swings as if the back tee did not exist. This drill is great for the hitter struggling with the swing track. A poor swing track will cause the bat to hit the back tee as the bat comes to the plate.

On all drills, make sure to concentrate on your footwork and balance. Without these you will never become a good hitter. Remember, no matter how much time you spend on drills, there is no substitute for actual game swings. Whenever working on the swing, take your time and work each swing just as if a pitch were coming in a game. Do not rush; bat habits form when rushing to get the work in.

*The double tee drill*

# Rules and Definitions

**Base on Balls:** When a hitter is allowed first base because the umpire has ruled four pitches to be out of the strike zone during that turn at bat, before the hitter hits the ball in play or swings at three strikes.

**Batted Ball:** A batted ball is any ball that hits the bat or is hit by a swing of the bat and hits in fair or foul territory. The hitter does not have to make an attempt to hit the ball for it to hit the bat and be a batted ball.

**Batter's Box:** The batter's box is the area in which the batter stands when at bat. The lines marking the box are also considered part of the batter's box.

**Batting Order:** This is the official listing of offensive players, the order in which members of that team must come to bat. Uniform number and defensive position must be listed on the lineup card. This lineup is delivered to the home plate umpire before the start of the game.

**Bunt:** A bunt is a ball that is intentionally tapped by the bat, slowly and near the plate. A bunt must stay in the infield, and never be an infield fly. Occasionally a hitter will take a full swing and barely make contact; this is referred to as a swinging bunt. A sacrifice bunt is performed when the hitter intentionally turns the body to tap the ball fair for the purpose of advancing the base runner to the next base, with no intention of reaching base themselves. A drag bunt is when the hitter tries to hide the bunt from the defense and taps the ball fair at the last second, attempting to reach first on a base hit.

**Catch:** A catch is a legally caught ball, which happens when the fielder catches the batted ball. A fielder needs to hold the ball long enough for the umpire to feel the fielder has control of the ball. If a player drops the ball after reaching into the glove to remove it or while throwing the ball, it is still a valid catch. The ball can be held by any part of the fielder's body, as long as complete control of the ball is provided. The fielder's feet must be in play, but do not need to be in fair territory.

**Illegal Catch:** This occurs when a fielder catches a batted or thrown ball with anything other than the hands or body or glove in the proper playing area. Should the catcher catch the fly ball with the catcher's mask, for example, it is illegal and the batter is not out.

**Dead Ball:** This occurs when a ball touches any object or player out of play, when a ball is caught in umpire's gear or offensive player's clothes. The umpire rules a dead ball if a ball crosses the dead ball line.

**Fair Ball:** A batted ball, which is judged according to the position of the ball to the foul line to be in fair territory. The fair ball is not affected by the position of the defensive player. As long as a ball stays inside the fair ball lines on the infield or passes over 3rd or 1st base and then travels into foul territory it is fair. This ball that passes over the base must have made contact with fair territory before traveling into foul ground.

**Fielder:** Any player on the defense that is playing in the field while the offense is hitting. Al fielders have to have their feet in fair territory at the time of the pitch. After the pitcher releases the pitch, the fielder may leave fair territory.

**Fly Ball:** This is a ball that travels into the air at contact from the bat.

**Foul Ball:** The ball that hits or is touched on or over foul territory between home and the first and third base; a ball that strikes a base runner while in foul territory; a ball that first hits or is touched in foul territory, beyond the first or third base; a ball that makes contact with the hitter after hitting the bat while the hitter is still in the batter's box, a ball that does not travel higher than the hitter's head after contact and hits the catcher or is caught by the catcher.

**Foul Tip:** A ball that is hit by the bat and goes directly from the bat, not higher than the batter's head, to the catcher's hand or glove and is legally caught by the catcher.

**Home Team:** This is the team that is decided by location of the game or coin flip. The home team bats second, meaning at the bottom of the inning.

**Illegally Batted Ball:** An illegally batted ball occurs when a hitter makes contact with the pitched ball when out of the batter's box. Also when the hitter makes contact with the ball while touching home plate, and when the hitter hits a ball with a bat that has been deemed illegal by the umpire. Also when the hitter makes contact with the ball after leaving the batter's box during the pitch and returning to the batter's box to make contact with the ball.

**Infield:** The infield is the portion of the field in fair territory that includes areas normally covered by infielders.

**Infield Fly:** A fair ball, not a line drive or an attempted bunt, that is or could be caught by an infielder with ordinary effort when there is a runner on 1st and 2nd or bases loaded with less than two outs. Any defensive player who takes a position in the infield at the start of the pitch shall be considered an infielder. The infield fly is ruled when the ball reaches the highest point of flight nearest an infielder. The ball is a live ball and runners may advance at the risk of the ball being caught. The runners can tag up and advance once the batted ball is touched by or caught by a fielder. The ball does not have to be caught by the infielder to be judged an infield fly. The hitter is out, to take away the chance for the hitter to run one of the runners off the base they are on at the time of the pitch.

**Inning:** An inning is the portion of the game in which one team is hitting. This is considered one half of an inning. The team is allowed three outs. At the end of the third out the opposite team will hit for three outs, and the inning is then completed.

**Line Drive:** A line drive is a ball that is batted sharply and directly at a defensive player. A line drive is hit hard and in a straight direction. A line drive cannot be called an infield fly.

**Offensive Team:** The offensive team is the team at bat. The only way to score a run is to be on the offensive.

**On Deck Batter:** This is the offensive player next up to hit. The player is normally practicing swings in foul territory near the batter's box, but out of the way of play.

**Outfield:** This is the fielder that defends the area in the field referred to as right field, left-field, or center field. These defensive players may be moved to an infield position in an emergency, and are also allowed to catch balls in the infield if necessary.

**Overthrow:** This happens when a thrown ball from a fielder goes past another position player who was intended to catch it. This ball will usually leave the field of play, but could be stopped by another player if they are hustling and backing up the throw. Quite often the runners will advance to the next base on this throwing error.

**Passed Ball:** This is a legally thrown ball from the pitcher to the plate which is missed by the catcher and a runner on base advances to the next base. This pitched ball needs to be close enough to the catcher that it is reasonable to think the catcher could have caught the pitch.

**Wild Pitch:** This is a legally thrown ball from the pitcher to the catcher, which is thrown so poorly that the catcher could not catch the pitch with reasonable effort.

**Play Ball:** This term is used by the plate umpire to indicate that play shall start; this call cannot be declared until all defensive players are in fair territory except the catcher. The catcher must be in the catcher's box behind the plate. All runners must be on the proper base.

**Quick Pitch:** This is a pitch made by the pitcher with the obvious attempt to catch the batter off balance. This pitch is made before the batter takes a desired position in the batter's box or while the batter is still getting prepared from the last pitch.

**Runner:** A runner is an offensive player that has reached base and has not yet been tagged, forced, or ruled out by the umpire. A hitter becomes a runner just as soon as they make contact with the ball and it is ruled fair. A hitter will also be ruled a runner as soon as the umpire rules ball four and a walk is issued.

**Sacrifice Fly:** A sacrifice fly is scored when, with fewer than two outs, the hitter scores a runner with a fly ball or a line drive that is caught by the defense. A sacrifice fly is not ruled when a runner advances to any other base but home on a fly ball.

**Starting Player:** This is a player listed on the lineup card given to the home plate umpire before the game starts. This player does not have to play the entire game, only start the first pitch of the game.

**Stealing:** Stealing is the act of a runner attempting to advance to the next base during a pitch to the plate. If the scorekeeper rules no attempt was made to catch the runner stealing, this could be called defensive indifference and no steal recorded, but the runner does not return to the previous base.

**Strike Zone:** When the hitter sets up in the hitting position called the stance, the space over any part of the home plate between the batter's knees to the batter's letters is the area called the strike zone. A hitter may attempt a swing at any pitch, but this area is the area an umpire may rule a strike without a swing taken by the hitter.

**Substitute:** Any player from the roster that is not listed on the opening pitch lineup, who at some point in the game replaced another teammate. A player not listed on the lineup card as an extra is not eligible to play in the game as a starter or substitute.

**Trapped Ball:** A fly ball or line drive that hits the ground or fence before being caught. A thrown ball to any base for a force out which is caught with the glove after touching the ground. The glove must be under the ball to prevent the ball from making contact with the ground prior to landing in the glove.

**Time:** A term used by the umpire to stop play for any reason. At this point no advance by the offense or defense can occur. Time will be called by the umpire when something or someone interferes with play. A player can request time, but the umpire may or may not allow an interruption in play.

**Triple Play:** This is a play by the defense in which three outs are recorded by the defense in one play with three offensive players being called out on one hit ball.

**Turn At Bat:** An at-bat begins when a player first enters the batter's box and continues until the payer is substituted for, ruled out by the umpire, or becomes a runner after making contact with the pitched ball.

# INDEX